LOURDES UBIETA

★★★★★★★★★★★★★★

THE POWER OF THE LATINO VOTE

© Lourdes Ubieta, 2024

linkscgroup@gmail.com

Design, layout and cover

Janet Salgado M.
Editor

janet.salgado@gmail.com

Illustrated fonts taken from Freepik

ISBN: 9798340535351

Independently published

Dedication

To my parents, who chose to be immigrants rather than slaves.

To Gabriel, my American-born son.

To the United States for adopting me: This country is not a dream. It is a miracle.

And to all the immigrants who, after many sacrifices and perseverance, today have a voice and a vote.

Acknowledgment

To Santiago, for believing in me every step of our journey.

Index

Dedication 7

Acknowledgment 9

Introduction 17

Prologue 19

Chapter 1

The demographic evolution of latinos in the United States

Population growth of the latino community in the United States from the late 20th century to the present 27

Late 20th century: The Foundation of latino growth 27

The 21st century boom: Beyond immigration 28

Geographic distribution: Beyond the southwest 29

Implications of growth: Power and influence 29

Migration, birth, and assimilation factors that have driven this growth 30

Migration: The gateway to the United States 30

Economic factors in the countries of origin 30

Political and social factors 31

Immigration policies in the United States 31

Birth rates: The internal driver of growth 32

Assimilation: Adapting without losing identity 32

Latinos are the largest minority in the United States 33

Latino electoral participation: The great challenge 35

2020 Presidential Election 35

Midterm Elections (2018 and 2022) 36

Chapter 2
The geography of the latino vote

States with the largest concentrations of latino voters 39
  California: The state with the largest latino population 39
  Texas: The second state with the most latino voters 41
  Florida: A battleground state with latino diversity 43
  New York: The importance of the Puerto Rican and Dominican vote 45
  Arizona: A swing state with a growing latino population 46
  New Mexico: The highest proportion of latinos in the U.S. 48
Differences between states in terms of participation and voting trends 49
  Factors affecting voter participation 49
  Voting trends by state 50
  Cultural differences and key issues in participation and voting trends ... 52
  Florida as an example of political transition 52
Expansion of the latino vote in non-traditionally latino states: Georgia, North
Carolina, and Nevada 56
  Georgia: The rapid growth of the latino vote in the southeast 56
  North Carolina: A transition state with a growing latino population 57
  Nevada: The latino vote transforming a purple state 59
Pennsylvania: The crown jewel of swing States? 60
  The latino vote in Pennsylvania: Importance and analysis 60
  Latino population in Pennsylvania 60
  Geographic distribution of the latino vote in Pennsylvania 61
  The weight of the latino vote in Pennsylvania 61
  Voting trends of latino voters in Pennsylvania 62
  Factors driving latino voter mobilization in Pennsylvania ....

Chapter 3
History of the latino vote in the United States

The evolution of the latino vote (1998-2023) 65
  1998-2000: Early signs of latino vote growth 65
  2004 Presidential Election: Consolidation of the latino vote 66
  2006 Midterm Elections: Immigration as a central issue 66
  2008 Presidential Election: The OBAMA era 66
  2010 Midterm Elections: Challenges for democrats 67
  2012 Presidential Election: The Re-election of BARACK H. OBAMA 68
  2014 Midterm Elections: Low latino participation 68
  2016 Presidential Election: The impact of TRUMP 69

Index

2018 Midterm Elections 69
2020 Presidential Election: Record participation 69
2022 Midterm Elections: Increasing diversification of the latino vote 70
Emerging trends: Young latino voters and changes in participation among different latino subgroups 72
The rise of young latino voters: The generation defining the future......... 72
Changes in participation among different latino subgroups.................... 73
a. Mexicans: The largest and most diverse latino group 74
b. Cubans: A conservative Group in evolution 74
c. Puerto Ricans: A growing electoral power in the northeast and Florida ... 75
d. Venezuelans: An emerging group with conservative leanings................ 76

Chapter 4
The U.S. electoral system

Origin of the U.S. electoral system and the electoral college.......................... 79
Why was the Electoral College created?..................................... 79
How does the Electoral College work? 80
Difference between the popular vote and the Electoral College 80
Impact of the latino vote on the Electoral College 80
What if no candidate reaches the majority of electoral votes? The contingent election... 81
How is a contingent election resolved? 81
Examples of contingent elections in U.S. history 81
Reforms and controversies... 82
The Conventions 82
Caucuses 84
Primary elections 85
Independent (nonpartisan) voting in the United States 86
Religion and the Latino Vote 90

Chapter 5
Coming out of the shadows

The RONALD REAGAN era 95
The rise of the latino vote 96
Behavior of the latino vote: From REAGAN to BIDEN 96
1980 Election (RONALD REAGAN vs. JIMMY CARTER)........................... 97
1984 Election (RONALD REAGAN vs. WALTER MONDALE) 97
1992 Election (BILL CLINTON vs. GEORGE H. W. BUSH vs. ROSS PEROT)............. 97

2000 Election (George W. Bush vs. Al Gore) 98
2008 Election (Barack Obama vs. John McCain) 98
2016 Election (Donald Trump vs. Hillary Clinton) 98
2020 Election (Joe Biden vs. Donald Trump) 99
The latino vote decides 99
2000 Presidential Election: Florida and Cuban Americans 100
2008 Presidential Election 100
2012 Presidential Election: Colorado and Nevada 101
2016 Presidential Election: Florida and Texas 102
2020 Presidential Election: Arizona and Nevada 102
The latino vote grows and multiplies 103
Voting patterns and diversity 103
States where the latino vote carries more weight 104
Political campaigns: Adjustments to win the latino vote 106
Investment in the latino vote vs. the anglo vote 110
Examples of specific campaigns targeting latino voters and their impact on the
results 111
Barack Obama's 2012 Campaign: "Latinos for Obama" 111
Donald Trump's 2020 Campaign: "Latinos for Trump" 112
Joe Biden's 2020 Campaign: "Todos con Biden" 113
Hillary Clinton's 2016 Campaign: "I'm with her" 114
I'm switching parties! Latinos and party affinity 114
How to win the latino vote 115
Political representation of latinos in elected offices 118
Florida: Growth of latino representation 118
New York: Advances in latino representation 118
Nevada: Growing representation 119
California: A leader in latino representation 119
Arizona: Growth of latino representation 120
Pennsylvania: Growing latino representation 120
The future of the latino vote: Challenges and opportunities 121

Chapter 6
Florida: Model of latino vote power

Cuban immigration 126
The first wave: Refugees after the Cuban revolution (1960-1970) 127
The Mariel crisis (1980) 127
The Balsero crisis (1994) 128
Impact of "wet-foot, dry-foot" 128

Index

End of "wet-foot, dry-foot" (2017) 128
Current crisis and recent waves 2024 129
Cuban-American political power 129
   LINCOLN DIAZ-BALART 129
   MARIO DIAZ-BALART 130
   ILEANA ROS-LEHTINEN 130
   MEQUIADES "Mel" MARTINEZ 131
   MARCO RUBIO 131
   Other Cuban-Americans in high U.S. politics 132
      BOB MENÉNDEZ 132
      TED CRUZ 132
      ALBIO SIRES 132
      NICOLE MALLIOTAKIS 132
   The political legacy and future of Cuban-Americans 133
The political crisis in Venezuela and its impact on migration to the United States ... 133
   The political and economic collapse in Venezuela 133
   Increase in Venezuelan migration to the United States 134
   The impact of the Venezuelan community in the United States 135
The decisive Puerto Rican vote in Florida 135
   Puerto Rican voter demographics 135
   Senator RICK SCOTT's Victory, Puerto Rico decided! 136

Conclusions 137

Introduction

I am an immigrant and have been a witness, for more than two decades, to the rise of the Latino vote as a determining force in U.S. politics, which has motivated me to write these pages.

This book is addressed to everyone, immigrants and non-immigrants alike, regardless of race, creed, or political affiliation. I explore the evolution of the Latino vote, starting from when President Ronald Reagan, through his immigration reform, brought millions of Latinos out of the shadows.

Latino voters are no longer a marginal group. We are a crucial tool of political and social power, though we still do not participate to the extent we could and should. We are the largest minority in the most powerful country in the world, yet we vote in lower proportions than other minorities. This is a topic we must reflect upon and change.

In these pages, I address the electoral battles that have been decided by the Latino vote, demonstrating the real impact we can have when we participate. I also explore the role of religion in our voting decisions, a factor that, for many Latinos, guides their family priorities and principles.

I also analyze how Latin American dictatorships have influenced the political mindset of millions of Hispanic voters, reflecting on our responsibility in deciding the future of the United States, a country that must not resemble the ones many of us had to flee from.

Additionally, I highlight the role of important Latino figures who have made history in American politics, whose service has marked a before and after for our community.

17

This book is also a call to participation. We cannot allow ourselves to be manipulated in our intentions, nor should we vote without being well-informed. The Latino vote must be thoughtful, considered, and always guided by the well-being of our families and our values.

Assimilating into life in the United States does not mean losing our identity or principles. I firmly believe that very soon we will see a President of the United States with a Hispanic last name, and I am sure they will excel and be a source of pride for both Latinos and non-Latinos.

I hope you enjoy this book, find it useful, and that through these pages, you find the motivation to contribute actively and legally to building the future of the United States.

Prologue

There is no doubt that Hispanics have become an important electoral force in the United States. According to projections from the Pew Center, in 2024, 36.2 million Hispanics will be eligible to vote, representing 14.7 % of the entire electorate. Furthermore, the Hispanic vote will be decisive in the majority of the so-called "swing states"–Arizona, North Carolina, Georgia, Nevada, and Pennsylvania; those states that will determine who wins the presidential election.

Democrats were convinced that with the growth of the Hispanic electorate, the Democratic Party would become the majority party in the country. For decades, Democrats dominated the Hispanic vote, with their presidential candidates consistently winning it by wide margins, 3 to 1 or 2 to 1.

But this Democratic hope vanished with the arrival of DONALD TRUMP on the national scene. TRUMP managed to make inroads with Hispanics, primarily through the populist economic policies he promoted during his administration, which benefited millions of working Hispanic families. Not only did the unemployment rate for Hispanics drop to a historic low, but their wages and household income increased significantly. Thus, in 2020, despite not being reelected, TRUMP's support among Hispanic voters increased by 10 points nationally, from 28 % in 2016 to a significant 38 %.

With the overwhelming embrace of TRUMP's "America First" policies by the majority of Republican leadership in favor of the working class, the shift of Hispanic voters toward the Republican Party gained momentum. In the

19

2022 midterm elections, the Hispanic vote for Republican candidates for the House of Representatives reached 39 %, the highest level since 1978 and ten points higher than in 2018.

In key states, Republicans also performed extraordinarily well. Governor DeSantis won the majority of the Hispanic vote, not only winning the Cuban vote in Miami-Dade County but also the Puerto Rican vote in Osceola County, which had been largely dominated by Democrats. In North Carolina, Congressman Ted Budd won his Senate race, receiving 46 % of the Hispanic vote. Even in Arizona, although Republican Blake Masters did not prevail in his Senate bid, his candidacy received 40 % of the Hispanic vote, ten points higher than what his Republican colleague Martha McSally received in 2018 in her race for the same position.

It is evident that Democratic strategists assumed Hispanics would continue voting with a group mentality, identifying mostly with the Democratic Party. They did not realize that over time, the Hispanic population has been fully integrating into the country's culture, ceasing to be monolithic in terms of their political preferences. Today, Hispanics vote like the rest of American voters, thinking about their individual interests and what is best for their particular family. For this reason, they are open to breaking with Democrats to vote for Trump and other Republican candidates whose policies are more attractive to them.

In this sense, it is worth noting that the change in Hispanic electoral trends also reflects the discomfort many Hispanics feel with the far-left extremism that the Democratic Party has recently adopted. The radical stances taken by Democrats, such as allowing transgender men to compete in girls' sports and have access to their bathrooms and locker rooms, or defunding the police, repel a large sector of the Hispanic electorate. And no matter how much Democratic activists continue to tell them that the Democratic Party is the "party of Hispanics," Hispanic voters today have the independence of thought to not be swayed by those condescending arguments and to vote according to their principles and common sense for a Republican candidate, even if it's for the first time.

There are not many people who can fully understand and clearly explain the complexities of the Hispanic community in the United States and the growing political power they are acquiring. My longtime friend, the

Prologue

distinguished journalist and commentator LOURDES UBIETA, is one of those people who can help us objectively understand the Hispanic political phenomenon, overcoming the typical clichés and generalities that are often made about Hispanics. For decades, LOURDES has been at the forefront of the discussion of the major challenges our nation faces and the impact they have on the Hispanic community, interviewing the most relevant figures in politics, economics, and culture in the country, and speaking with Hispanic citizens of all kinds and social origins.

In this, her new book, *The Power of the Latino Vote in the United States*, LOURDES will take us by the hand to deeply understand what the rise of Hispanics to political relevance means in the most powerful nation in the world.

ALFONSO AGUILAR

Director of Hispanic Outreach at the American Principles Project and former head of the U.S. Office of Citizenship under President GEORGE W. BUSH'S administration.

Chapter 1

Chapter 1

The **demographic** *evolution of* **latinos** *in the* **United States**

To understand the power of the Latino vote in the United States, we first need to take a short journey through the demographic evolution of this vibrant community. In recent decades, the Latino population has not only grown but has gone from being a relatively small minority to becoming the largest in the country. This growth has not been a linear or simple process, but rather a reflection of multiple factors such as migration, the birth of new generations, and the integration of Latinos into all aspects of American life.

Just a few decades ago, in the 80s and 90s, the Latino community was primarily seen as an emerging group, mostly concentrated in certain areas of the southwestern United States, such as California, Texas, and Florida. At that time, most Latinos living in the country were first or second-generation immigrants, many from Mexico, Puerto Rico, and Cuba. Today, things have changed significantly. Not only has the Latino-origin population increased, but new generations born in the United States have begun to occupy important spaces in society, and of course, in politics.

To get an idea of the scope of this growth, we only need to look at the figures. According to the 2020 census, more than 62 million people in the United States identify as Latinos or Hispanics, which represents approximately 19% of the country's total population. This is a significant increase compared to the 35 million Latinos recorded in the 2000 census. This demographic growth has had a direct impact on the political power of Latinos, as more people means more voters, and more voters mean greater influence in political decisions.

But the growth of the Latino community has not been uniform. While California remains the state with the largest number of Latinos, states like Texas, Florida, Arizona, and New Mexico have seen equally notable growth. In recent decades, we have also witnessed the expansion of the Latino vote in states that traditionally were not associated with this community, such as Georgia, North Carolina, and Nevada. These new Latino population centers have played a key role in changing the electoral dynamics in those places, which we will see in more detail in later chapters.

Now, when we talk about the Latino population in the United States, it is important to note that it is not a monolithic group. Latinos come from a diversity of countries and cultures, and although they share certain elements such as language, each group has its own history and immigration experience. For example, most of the Latinos in the United States have Mexican roots, but there are also large Puerto Rican, Cuban, Salvadoran, Dominican, and Colombian communities, to name a few. This diversity is also reflected in electoral behavior, where political preferences can vary according to the country of origin, migration history, and the generation to which they belong.

Mexicans are by far the largest group within the Latino community in the United States, representing more than 60% of Latinos in the country. This is one of the reasons why states like California and Texas, with a large Mexican-origin population, are considered key in terms of the Latino vote. Puerto Ricans, on the other hand, are more concentrated in states like New York and Florida, while Cubans, especially in Florida, have played a very important role in presidential elections due to their strong political participation.

As the Latino community has grown, its profile in terms of age has also changed. Today, Latinos are, on average, a much younger population than other groups in the United States. This youth is one of the reasons why the power of the Latino vote continues to expand: every year, thousands of young Latinos turn 18 and join the electoral roll, bringing new perspectives and energy to American politics.

The demographic growth of Latinos in the United States has undoubtedly been one of the most important phenomena of recent decades. And with this growth comes greater responsibility and a greater capacity to influence the future of the country. In the next chapters, we will explore how this expansion has been key to shaping the political landscape, and how, in many cases, Latinos have been decisive in the election of the most important leaders in the United States.

But for now, suffice it to say that the Latino community has come a long way, and its influence will only continue to grow in the coming years. As we will see in the following pages, demographic evolution is not just a story of numbers, but a story of people, families, and communities who have found a home in the United States and who are increasingly committed to its future.

Population growth of the latino community in the United States from the late 20th century to the present

The population growth of the Latino community in the United States from the late 20th century to the present is one of the most prominent and transformative demographic phenomena in the country's recent history. This growth has been not only quantitative, with an increase in the total number of Latinos, but also qualitative, with significant changes in the composition, geographic distribution, and social and political influence of the community.

Late 20th century: The foundation of latino growth

In the years following World War II, the Latino population in the United States was relatively small, although in some areas of the country, especially in the Southwest, it was already significant. The community was mostly composed of people of Mexican, Puerto Rican, and Cuban origin, and their presence was concentrated in states like California, Texas, Florida, and New York.

However, starting in the 1970s and 1980s, several factors contributed to a steady and sustained increase in the Latino population. Immigration reforms, such as the Immigration Act of 1965, which eliminated restrictive racial quotas, opened the doors to greater immigration from Latin America. Also, during this period, political and economic events in Latin American countries, such as economic crises in Mexico and Central America and dictatorships in countries like Cuba and Chile, drove people to migrate to the United States in search of safety and better opportunities.

By the late 20th century, in the 1990s, Latinos were already beginning to make their demographic presence felt in the United States. In the 2000 census, the Latino population in the United States exceeded 35 million, representing nearly 12% of the country's total population. This marked a turning point: the Latino community was not only growing at a faster rate than other demographic groups, but it was also beginning to attract the attention of politicians, businesspeople, and community leaders due to its potential influence on the country's future.

The 21st century boom: Beyond immigration

Throughout the 21st century, the growth of the Latino population has continued at an accelerated and sustained pace, although the dynamics have changed. Whereas in previous decades much of Latino growth was driven by immigration, in the 21st century this growth has been mostly determined by birth rates within the United States. Latinos are, on average, younger than other racial or ethnic groups in the country, which means they have higher birth rates, and the younger generations are born in the United States.

In the 2020 census, more than 62 million people identified as Latino or Hispanic, representing approximately 19% of the total population of the United States. This impressive growth has been driven by both immigration and high birth rates within the community. Unlike the early decades of the 20th century, when most Latinos were first-generation immigrants, today much of the Latino population in the United States is U.S.-born. This has created a new cultural dynamic, with a community that blends Latino traditions and roots with a deep connection to American society.

In addition to Mexicans, who make up more than 60% of the Latino population in the United States, other communities have grown significantly. Puerto Ricans, the second-largest Latino community, have increased their presence in the country, particularly in states like Florida and New York. Cubans, Dominicans, Salvadorans, Guatemalans, Colombians, and other Central and South American groups have also grown in number, contributing to the cultural richness and diversity of the overall Latino community.

Geographic distribution: Beyond the southwest

As the Latino population has grown, its geographic distribution has also changed. Traditionally, most Latinos in the United States were concentrated in the Southwest, in states like California, Texas, Arizona, and New Mexico, due to their proximity to Mexico and Central America. However, in recent decades, the Latino community has expanded to other states, including those that did not have a significant Latino presence in the past.

States like Florida and New York have seen a considerable increase in their Latino population, partly due to immigration from Cubans, Puerto Ricans, and Dominicans. More recently, states like Georgia, North Carolina, Nevada, and Pennsylvania have experienced rapid growth in their Latino populations. In some of these states, Latinos now play a crucial role in the political and economic sphere, changing the demographic profile of communities that were once predominantly white or African American.

This geographic growth has been driven by several factors. On one hand, the labor market has led Latinos to seek new opportunities in areas with growing economies, such as the South and Midwest. On the other hand, urbanization and the search for a better quality of life have also motivated many Latino families to settle in more suburban and rural areas, far from the large cities of the Southwest.

Implications of growth: Power and influence

The growth of the Latino population has had a profound impact on many aspects of American life, but perhaps the most significant change has been in the political arena. The increasing number of Latinos eligible to vote has attracted the attention of political parties, especially in swing states like Florida, Arizona, Nevada, and Colorado, where the Latino vote can decide the outcome of an election.

This growing power has not only been manifested at the ballot box but also in political representation. In the last two decades, we have seen a significant increase in the number of Latinos elected to public office at the local, state, and national levels. In Congress, for example, the number of Latino legislators has increased significantly, and more and more Latinos are occupying key positions in politics and public administration.

The cultural and economic impact of the Latino community has also been undeniable. Today, Latinos represent a crucial part of the workforce, especially in blue-collar sectors such as construction, agriculture, hospitality, and services. Additionally, the cultural influence of the Latino community can be seen in music, television, film, and other aspects of American popular culture.

Migration, birth, and assimilation factors that have driven this growth

The growth of the Latino community in the United States has been driven by several interrelated factors shaping its evolution over the past few decades. Among them are migration, birth rates, and the processes of assimilation into American life. Each of these factors has played a key role in increasing the Latino population and in strengthening its social, economic, and political influence in the country.

Migration: The gateway to the United States

Immigration has been the fundamental factor driving the growth of the Latino population in the United States, especially throughout the 20th century and the first decades of the 21st century. Over the years, millions of people have left their home countries in Latin America in search of better opportunities, safety, and a more promising future in the United States. But this migratory flow has not been uniform and has been influenced by various economic, political, and social factors both in the countries of origin and in the United States.

Economic factors in the countries of origin

One of the main drivers of migration has been the search for better economic opportunities. Throughout history, many Latin American countries have faced economic crises, high unemployment rates, poverty, and a lack of opportunities to improve quality of life. For example, the economic crisis in Mexico in the 80s and 90s, known as the "lost decade," led to a massive wave of migration to the United States. Mexican workers sought employment in agriculture, construction, and other sectors in the United States, where they could earn much more than in their home countries.

Similarly, Central American countries such as El Salvador, Guatemala, and Honduras have witnessed waves of migration to the United States due to a lack of economic opportunities and political instability. This migration has grown in recent decades, driven by poverty, gang violence, and corruption in their countries of origin.

Political and social factors

In addition to economic factors, political and social conditions have also played a crucial role in Latino migration to the United States. Countries like Cuba and Venezuela have experienced political crises that led to the migration of thousands of people in search of freedom and stability. In the case of Cuba, the 1959 Revolution and Fidel Castro's communist policies led many Cubans to flee to Florida and other states, establishing a solid and politically active community.

Similarly, the civil war in El Salvador (1980-1992) and the conflicts in Guatemala during the 70s and 80s resulted in an exodus of refugees and migrants seeking safety and asylum in the United States. The situation in Venezuela in recent years, marked by a deep economic and political crisis, has led to an increase in Venezuelan immigrants –mostly seeking– refuge and new opportunities.

Immigration policies in the United States

The growth of the Latino population has also been closely linked to U.S. immigration policies. Throughout the 20th century, there were periods when opportunities for legal immigration were facilitated, such as with the Bracero Program (1942-1964), which allowed hundreds of thousands of Mexican workers to temporarily enter the country to work in agriculture. Programs like this helped cement the migratory relationship between Mexico and the United States, creating family and labor networks that persist today.

In more recent years, stricter immigration policies and border crises have not completely stopped migration but have made it more complex. Despite the difficulties of migrating legally in some cases, many Latinos continue to come to the United States, both legally and illegally, due to the persistence of the factors driving migration in their home countries.

Birth rates: The internal driver of growth

While immigration was the dominant factor in the early waves of Latino growth in the United States, in recent decades, natural population increase (i.e., the number of births within the country) has significantly driven the growth of the community.

Latinos in the United States have maintained higher birth rates than other racial and ethnic groups, leading to rapid growth in the U.S.-born population. For example, during the 1990s and early 2000s, Latina women had a higher average birth rate than other groups of women in the United States, contributing to the faster growth of the Latino community.

For instance, by the 1990s, the birth rate for Latinos in the U.S. was approximately 27 births per 1,000 people according to data from the National Center for Health Statistics, while the rate for non-Hispanic whites was 14.4, and for African Americans, 20.3 per 1,000 people.

As more Latinos have been born in the United States, the dynamics of the community have also changed. In the past, a large part of Latinos were first-generation immigrants. Today, most Latinos in the United States are citizens born in the country. This has generated a community that is deeply rooted in American life, with generations of young Latinos who, while maintaining cultural and family ties to their countries of origin, primarily identify as Americans.

This increase in births has strengthened the demographic power of Latinos and has generated continuous growth of the community without relying as heavily on immigration. Additionally, the youth of the Latino population means that a large portion of this community is still of working age, studying, and, most importantly, voting, ensuring that Latino influence in the country will continue to grow.

Assimilation: Adapting without losing identity

The process of assimilation –the phenomenon by which immigrants and their descendants gradually adopt the customs, values, language, and norms of the host country– has been a key aspect of the growth and evolution of the Latino community in the United States. While immigration and birth rates have driven the numerical increase of Latinos, assimilation has shaped how this community integrates into American society without losing its cultural identity.

Assimilation in the United States has been a dynamic process, where Latinos adopt aspects of the dominant culture, such as the English language, while maintaining strong ties to their cultural roots. This duality has allowed Latinos not only to integrate into American society but also to enrich the country's culture with their own traditions, language, and values.

One of the main indicators of assimilation has been English proficiency among Latinos. Younger generations of U.S.-born Latinos tend to be fully bilingual, allowing them to navigate seamlessly between both worlds. However, despite the growing adoption of English, many Latinos continue to value and preserve the Spanish language, not only as a connection to their roots but also as an important tool in the labor market and daily life in an increasingly multicultural country.

The process of assimilation has also been reflected in the growing participation of Latinos in American politics, education, and the economy. As more U.S.-born Latinos have come of age, their presence in politics has increased. Latinos are participating more actively in elections, electing representatives from their community, and advocating for policies that reflect their interests.

Assimilation, however, has not meant the disappearance of Latino identity. Instead of full traditional assimilation, the Latino community has adopted a "biculturalism" approach, where they can adapt to American life without losing their cultural heritage. This balance between integration and cultural preservation has allowed the Latino community to grow and thrive while influencing the social and cultural fabric of the United States.

Latinos are the largest minority in the United States

Latinos have become the largest ethnic minority in the United States, surpassing African Americans and Asians in numbers.

According to the 2020 Census, Latinos became the largest minority group in the United States, surpassing other ethnic minorities in terms of population.

- **Latinos**: They constitute approximately 19 % of the total population, with more than 62.1 million people.

- **African Americans**: They represent 12.4 % of the U.S. population, with around 41 million people. Although African Americans were historically the largest minority group, Latinos surpassed them in the past two decades due to higher birth rates and immigration.
- **Asians**: They are approximately 7.2 % of the U.S. population, with about 24 million people. The Asian population has also grown rapidly, primarily driven by immigration, but it remains smaller than the Latino population.

Being the largest minority has had a profound social impact on the United States, which is felt in everyday life and has transformed many areas of daily life:

- **Cultural diversity**: The presence of Latinos has enriched the country's cultural diversity, with their influence visible in music, art, gastronomy, and media. Latino culture, particularly Mexican culture, has left a notable mark on national and local festivities, with celebrations such as Cinco de Mayo or Hispanic Heritage Month.
- **Changes in the young population**: Latinos are one of the youngest populations in the country, with a significantly lower median age than African Americans and Asians. This means they will have a growing impact on schools, universities, and the labor market in the coming decades.
- **Economy and workforce**: Latinos constitute a significant part of the workforce in key sectors such as construction, commerce, agriculture, and the service sector. They are also emerging as entrepreneurs in both urban and rural areas, leading to a boom in Latino-owned businesses.

Demographic growth has also strengthened the political power of Latinos, especially in "battleground" states like Arizona, Nevada, Texas, and Florida. Thus, there is a clear increase in political representation, with more Latinos being elected to public office at local, state, and federal levels in each election. Likewise, in recent presidential elections, the Latino vote has been a decisive factor in key states.

Of course, being the largest minority in the world's leading power also brings a series of challenges and responsibilities for Latinos, who ultimately become guarantors of the consolidation of American leadership in the free world.

Latinos must continue to mobilize to actively participate in the electoral process, both in terms of voting and in promoting policies that benefit the community. The low percentage of voter turnout in some segments remains a challenge.

Latinos also have the responsibility to fight for greater equity in education and access to economic opportunities. Although Latinos represent a significant portion of the workforce, they face challenges in terms of access to higher education and high-paying jobs.

As Latinos become a more influential bloc, they have the responsibility to foster community leadership, support Latino-owned small businesses, and continue to build a bridge between their cultures of origin and the dominant culture in the United States.

Latino electoral participation: The great challenge

Latino electoral participation in the United States has gradually increased over the past few decades, but it still faces major challenges. Despite being the largest minority in the country, Latino voter participation remains relatively low compared to other demographic groups.

Some factors, such as language barriers, a lack of clear information on how to vote, civic education about the importance of voting, the lack of engagement from younger Latinos, and inadequate community mobilization, are some of the explanations for electoral abstention.

2020 Presidential election

- **Latinos who voted**: Approximately 16.6 million Latinos voted in the 2020 presidential election, representing 13.3 % of the national electorate, according to data from NALEO (National Association of Latino Elected and Appointed Officials).

- **Increase in participation**: This represented a 30 % increase compared to 2016, when about 12.7 million Latinos voted.

- **Voter turnout rate**: The voter turnout rate was 53 % of eligible Latinos. This percentage was lower compared to the 67 % of non-Hispanic whites and 60 % of African Americans. Latinos made up about 19 % of the total U.S. population.

Midterm elections (2018 and 2022)

- In the 2018 midterm elections, it is estimated that about 40 % of eligible Latinos voted, a significant increase compared to previous midterm election cycles.
- In 2022, Latinos also participated in higher percentages in key states such as Arizona, Nevada, Texas, and Florida, but the exact participation data is still being analyzed.

As the Latino population continues to grow, the potential for its electoral impact increases. However, it will be essential to overcome current challenges to increase voter turnout and strengthen their political influence.

For the 2024 general elections, the National Association of Latino Elected and Appointed Officials (NALEO) has projected a strong impact from the Latino vote in the presidential elections.

According to their preliminary analysis, it is expected that:

1. **Number of latino voters**: About 17.5 million Latinos could vote in the 2024 elections, representing a continuation of the growth in Latino electoral participation. This is an increase compared to the 16.6 million who voted in 2020.

2. **Proportion of the electorate**: Latinos will make up about 15 % of the total electorate. This continues to consolidate Latinos as the largest minority voting bloc in the country.

3. **Key states**: Latinos will continue to be decisive in battleground states like Arizona, Nevada, Texas, Florida, and Georgia, where vote margins are often narrow. Their participation could be crucial in tipping the balance toward one party or another.

4. **Mobilization of young people**: One important factor in participation will be the mobilization of young Latinos, who make up a large part of the Latino electorate. Many of them are reaching voting age, which could influence outcomes in several key states.

5. **Priority issues**: The economy, immigration, health, and education will remain key issues that will mobilize Latino voters in 2024.

In general, NALEO expects the Latino community to play an even more important role in the outcome of the 2024 elections, consolidating its political influence across the country.

Chapter 2

The *geography* of the *latino vote*

The Latino vote in the United States has gained critical relevance due to the growth of the Latino population and their increasing participation in the country's political system. However, its impact varies considerably depending on the geographic region in which it is located. This geographic diversity affects both local and state elections, as well as presidential elections, since Latinos represent different percentages of the electoral population depending on the state, and their concerns and voting patterns may change based on local factors, such as the economy, immigration, and security.

States with the largest concentrations of latino voters

Latino voters in the United States are one of the most influential forces in the country's politics, with an increasing number of citizens of Latino origin actively participating in elections. This growing participation has been crucial in swaying key elections at the federal and state levels. Among the states with the largest concentrations of Latino voters are California, Texas, Florida, New York, Arizona, and New Mexico, where Latino communities have had a significant impact on the political landscape. Below is a detailed analysis of the influence and distribution of Latino voters in these states:

California: The state with the largest latino population

Latino population
California home to approximately 15.6 million Latinos, representing nearly 40 % of the state's total population. Approximately 8.5 million of them are eligible to vote, surpassing any other state in terms of Latino voting population.

Distribution

Latino voters in California are primarily concentrated in urban areas and the Central Valley. Latinos of Mexican origin make up most of the Latino population in California.

- **Los Angeles and Southern California**: This region is home to one of the largest Latino populations in the state. In Los Angeles the Latino community is very diverse, and includes Mexicans, as well as Central and South Americans. Los Angeles County has the highest concentration of Latinos in any County in the country.
- **Central Valley**: Agricultural areas such as Fresno, Bakersfield, and Stockton have a considerable Latino population, and is known for both its high proportion of Latino voters and inconsistent voter turnout.
- **Bay Area**: Cities like San Francisco, Oakland, and San Jose also have a significant Latino population, although not as dominant as in other parts of California. Here, the diversity includes a middle and upper-class population, as well as more traditional communities.
- **San Diego**: Although not as large as Los Angeles, San Diego has a considerable Latino community, especially in areas like Chula Vista and National City.
- **Inland Empire**: Cities like Riverside and San Bernardino have a growing Latino population, influenced by proximity to Los Angeles and urban expansion.
- **Northern California**: Although in smaller proportion than in the south, cities like Sacramento also have a notable Latino population, influenced by state politics and the global economy.

Political impact

Latinos in California tend to overwhelmingly support the Democratic Party, which has contributed to the state being considered a Democratic stronghold. This preference is based on several factors, including immigration policies, healthcare access, and other social issues where Democrats have been perceived as more "aligned" with the concerns of the Latino community.

Their support has been key in presidential and state elections, influencing issues such as immigration reform, healthcare access, and labor rights. The influence of Latinos has also been decisive in the election of Latino politicians to Congress and other state offices, such as Alex Padilla, a senator from California, and Xavier Becerra, former attorney general of the state, and a secretary of Health and Human Services of the U.S.

Texas: The second state with the most latino voters

Latino population

Texas has a Latino population of more than 11.4 million, representing more than 40 % of the state's total population. Approximately 5.8 million Latinos are eligible to vote, meaning Latinos now represent the largest ethnic group in the state, surpassing non-Hispanic whites in terms of total population.

Distribution

Latino voters in Texas are distributed throughout the state, with notable presence in certain urban areas that reflect not only the migration history and proximity to Mexico but also the economic opportunities and immigration policies that have brought this population to different parts of the state. This distribution is crucial in electoral dynamics, especially in districts where Latinos can significantly influence local and state elections.

- **San Antonio**: Known for its rich Hispanic heritage, San Antonio has a significant Latino population, with more than 60 % of its population of Hispanic origin. This city is a Democratic stronghold in a predominantly Republican state, reflecting the influence of Latino voters.

- **Rio Grande Valley**: This area, which includes cities like McAllen, Brownsville, and Harlingen, is one of the regions with the highest concentration of Latino voters in Texas. Proximity to the Mexican border influences the demographics and political concerns of the community.

- **Houston:** As the largest city in Texas, Houston hosts a considerable Latino population, especially in areas like East Houston and certain parts of the southwest. Houston's diversity also includes a significant Mexican, Central American, and South American community.

- **Dallas-Fort Worth Metroplex**: Although more diversified, this area also has a rapidly growing Latino population, with neighborhoods and communities where Latinos are the majority or have a strong presence.

- **Austin**: The capital of Texas has seen an increase in its Latino population, especially in areas like East Austin, where the community has historically been significant.
- **Corpus Christi**: With a population that is about 60 % Latino, Corpus Christi is another city where Latino voters have considerable influence.
- **Lubbock and the Panhandle**: Although less known, even in more rural areas and toward the north of Texas, such as Lubbock, there is a growing and politically active Latino presence.

Political impact

Texas is traditionally considered a predominantly Republican state, although the state's political dynamics have shown signs of change in recent years. Historically, Texas has been a Republican stronghold, especially in presidential elections and the composition of its state legislature. However, there are several factors indicating an evolution in demographics and political preferences:

- **Demographics**: The population of Texas has been changing, with Latinos outnumbering non-Hispanic whites, which could influence political trends if Latinos' historical inclination toward the Democratic Party continues.
- **Recent electoral trends**: Although Texas voted for Donald Trump in the 2016 and 2020 elections, the vote margin has decreased with each recent election, suggesting a possible opening for Democrats. In the 2020 elections, Joe Biden reduced the gap compared to Hillary Clinton's results in 2016.
- **State legislation and politics**: Despite these demographic and electoral changes, Texas' state government remains dominated by Republicans, indicating that although there is a trend toward greater competition, Texas still behaves predominantly as a Republican state in terms of governance and legislation.

The Latino vote has also been decisive in the election of Hispanic-origin candidates such as U.S. Senator Ted Cruz, former Congresswoman for the 34th District Mayra Flores, Congressman Tony Gonzales, who represents Texas'

23rd Congressional District, one of the largest and most diverse districts in the country, Joaquin Castro, Congressman for the 20th District, and Sylvia Garcia, representing Houston's 29th District, among several others.

Florida: A battleground state with latino diversity

Latino population

In Florida, Latinos constitute 26 % of the state's total population, with more than 5.6 million Latino residents. Approximately 3.1 million are eligible to vote.

Distribution

Florida has experienced notable growth in its Latino population, with a 14.6 % increase between 2010 and 2020, surpassing national growth. This population is distributed throughout the state but with specific concentrations in certain areas.

- **Miami-Dade** leads with a Latino population of approximately 1.86 million, representing 68.7% of its total population. Cubans make up a large part of the population here, although there is also a growing Venezuelan and Central American community.
- **Orange County** (Orlando) has about 473,000 Latinos, 33.1 % of its population.
- **Broward County** follows with approximately 609,000 Latinos, 31.3 % of its population.
- **Hillsborough County** (Tampa) has 427,000 Latinos, representing 29.3 % of its population.

Political impact

Florida is a crucial state in presidential elections, and Latino voters, especially Cuban-Americans in South Florida, tend to support the Republican Party. This group has played a key role in tilting elections in favor of Republicans in recent elections.

However, in areas like Orlando, Latinos of Puerto Rican and South American origin tend to lean toward the Democratic Party, making the Latino vote in Florida one of the most diverse and competitive in the country.

Florida is known for its close elections and being a key state in presidential elections due to its 29 (now 30) electoral votes. In 2000, the presidential election between George W. Bush and Al Gore was decided in Florida, highlighting its importance. In recent elections, especially since 2020, there has been a significant strengthening of the Republican Party in Florida. Former President Donald Trump won the state in 2020, and in the 2022 elections, there was a significant Republican wave, with the Republican Party obtaining a supermajority in the state legislature. Currently, there are one million more registered Republican voters than Democrats in Florida, indicating a significant shift in the state's electoral demographics.

- **Diversity of origins**: Although historically Cubans have been a significant part of the Latino population in Florida, especially in Miami-Dade, diversity has increased. Communities of Mexicans, Puerto Ricans, Venezuelans, and other Latino groups are now scattered throughout the state, reflecting a national trend toward greater ethnic diversity within the Latino community.

- **Demographic changes**: The Latino population in Florida has not only grown in number but has also influenced the demographics of urban and suburban areas. For example, in the Orlando and Tampa areas, the growth of the Latino population has been significant, affecting the redistricting of electoral districts and local politics.

- **Political and social implications**: The growing Latino population in Florida has impacted state politics, with increased representation and growing interest in the Latino community by politicians due to its electoral weight. Additionally, this ethnic diversity within the Latino community also implies a variety of political interests and concerns, ranging from the economy to immigration.

- **Impact on elections:** Although the percentages of the Latino vote in Florida are approximate, the impact is clear. In DeSantis' re-election in 2022, it was reported that he won 58% of the Latino vote, highlighting the substantive importance of this demographic group in state elections. The Latino vote in Florida has elevated important figures in the community who have undoubtedly set precedents in American politics; figures such as Ileana Ros-Lehtinen, the first Cuban-American woman in Congress, U.S. Senator Marco Rubio, and the brothers Lincoln and MARIO DIAZ-BALART –to name a few– are figures who have influenced the lives of all Latinos in the U.S.

New York: The importance of the puerto rican and dominican vote

Latino population

The Latino population in New York is approximately 5 million, and more than 2.4 million Latinos are eligible to vote.

Distribution

The Latino community in New York is notably diverse and concentrated in the metropolitan area, although there are certain areas where their presence is significantly high:

- **The Bronx**: Known for its high concentration of Latinos, especially Puerto Ricans, but also Dominicans and Mexicans. Neighborhoods like Mott Haven, Melrose, and the South Bronx have a strong Latino influence.

- **Brooklyn**: Here, the Latino community is very diverse. Sunset Park is famous for its Mexican population, while Bushwick and Williamsburg have a mix of Puerto Ricans, Dominicans, and other Latino groups.

- **Queens**: One of the most diverse counties in the United States. Jackson Heights, Elmhurst, and Corona are known for their Colombian, Ecuadorian, and Mexican communities, among others.

- **Manhattan**: Although better known for its global diversity, areas like Washington Heights have a strong Dominican presence, and East Harlem (Spanish Harlem) has historically been a Latino neighborhood, although it has experienced gentrification.

- **Staten Island**: Although less known for its Latino population compared to other boroughs, it has Central and South American communities, especially on the North Shore.

Political impact

Latinos in New York tend to overwhelmingly vote for the Democratic Party, which has made New York a reliably Democratic state in presidential and state elections. However, the diversity of the Latino vote is showing a trend of change, with increased support for Republican candidates.

Political figures such as ALEXANDRIA OCASIO-CORTEZ and ADRIANO ESPAILLAT, both of Latino descent, have gained prominence representing predominantly Latino districts in Congress, reflecting the political influence of this community.

Arizona: A swing state with a growing latino population

Latino population

Arizona is a "battleground" state. It has a Latino population of approximately 3.2 million, with 1.3 million Latinos eligible to vote, representing just over 33 % of the total population. In recent elections, there has been an increase in Latino voter turnout, with record numbers in the 2022 primaries, suggesting growing interest in the electoral process.

Distribution

Latinos in Arizona are spread throughout the state, but mostly concentrated in Phoenix and Tucson, with a large proportion of them being of Mexican origin.

- **Phoenix and Maricopa County**: Phoenix, as Arizona's largest city, has a significant Latino population. Maricopa County, which includes Phoenix, is one of the counties with the highest number of Latinos in the state, reflecting diversity that includes Mexicans, Central Americans, and other Latino groups.
- **Yuma**: Located in southwestern Arizona, near the California and Mexico borders, Yuma has a considerable Latino population, especially of Mexican origin, due to its proximity to the border.
- **Tucson and Pima County**: Tucson is another city with a strong Latino presence. Here, Mexican cultural influence is very pronounced, with a history that includes Spanish colonization and proximity to Mexico.
- **Santa Cruz County**: This county, which includes the city of Nogales, has one of the highest proportions of Latino population in the state due to its border location. Nogales is known for its cross-border trade and as an important entry point.
- **Mexico Border Region**: Areas near the border, such as San Luis and Lukeville, have a high concentration of Latinos, many of whom work on both sides of the border or have family ties in Mexico.

- **Agricultural communities**: In agricultural regions like the Yuma Valley and the Salinas area, Latino labor is crucial. These agricultural workers, often of Mexican origin, contribute significantly to the state's economy.

Political impact

Immigration and economic issues are key for Latino voters in Arizona, and grassroots mobilization efforts have been essential in increasing Latino participation in the state.

Arizona's history as a republican state

- From 1952 to 2016, Arizona predominantly voted for Republican candidates in all presidential elections, except for once in 1996 when it voted for Democrat BILL CLINTON.
- Iconic senators such as BARRY GOLDWATER and JOHN MCCAIN, both Republicans, represented Arizona for decades, consolidating the state's identity as a Republican stronghold in national politics.
- At the state level, Arizona has tended to elect mostly Republican governors and state legislators.

Recent shift toward democrats

- **2020 Presidential Election**: Arizona voted for Democrat JOE BIDEN, marking a significant change, as it was the first time since 1996 that a Democrat won in the state.
- **Election of Democratic Senators**: Arizona elected KYRSTEN SINEMA in 2018, the first Democratic senator from Arizona in more than 30 years. In 2020, Democrat MARK KELLY also won a Senate seat.

Factors driving the change

- **Growth of the latino population**: With an increase in the Latino population and a growing focus on issues such as immigration and civil rights, Democrats have gained support in urban areas like Phoenix and Tucson.
- **Independent voters**: Arizona has many independent voters, making it a more competitive state in recent elections.

New Mexico: The highest proportion of latinos in the U.S.

Latino population

In New Mexico, Latinos make up more than 49 % of the total population, with around 1.1 million Latinos living in the state. Approximately 600,000 are eligible to vote.

Distribution

The Latino community in New Mexico is spread throughout the state, with concentrations in Albuquerque, Santa Fe, and the southern part of the state. Most Latinos in New Mexico are of Mexican origin, and many have roots that date back several generations in the region.

The distribution of the Latino population in New Mexico not only reflects its colonial history and cultural blending with Native American populations but also internal and external migration. It is a diverse Latino community, including people of Mexican, Spanish, and other Latin American ancestry, with cultural influence permeating all aspects of life in the state.

- **Albuquerque**: New Mexico's largest city, Albuquerque, has a significant Latino population. This community is influential in the city's culture, politics, and economy, with neighborhoods like South Valley traditionally having a strong Hispanic presence.

- **Santa Fe**: As the state capital, Santa Fe also has a considerable Latino voter population intertwined with Native Americans, creating a unique mix.

- **Las Cruces**: Located in the southern part of the state, Las Cruces has a significant Latino population, influenced by its proximity to the Mexican border and the presence of New Mexico State University in Las Cruces.

- **Rural and Northern New Mexico**: Rural areas and northern parts of the state, such as Taos, Española, and the Chimayó Valleys, have Latino communities that have maintained Spanish traditions and dialects for over 400 years.

- **Border Region**: Although New Mexico does not have a direct border with Mexico, areas like the southwest of the state, near El Paso, Texas, reflect a cultural blend that includes a strong Latino presence due to proximity and historical and economic interactions with Mexico.

Political impact

New Mexico is predominantly a Democratic state, and Latinos have been a fundamental part of this coalition. Their influence has been key in state and federal elections, helping to elect Latino leaders such as former Governor Bill Richardson and maintaining Democratic control in Congress.

Issues such as education, healthcare, and immigrant rights are of great importance to Latino voters in New Mexico.

Differences between states in terms of participation and voting trends

In the United States, electoral participation and voting trends vary significantly between states due to a combination of historical, demographic, cultural, and political factors. Each state has unique characteristics that influence how its residents vote and how active they are in the electoral process. Below is a review of how these factors affect participation and voting trends in different states:

Factors affecting voter participation

a. Demographic population and ethnic composition

One of the most important factors affecting participation and voting trends in states is the demographic and ethnic composition of their population. States with large minority populations, such as Latinos, African Americans, and Asians, tend to have electoral participation patterns and political preferences that differ from states with predominantly white populations.

- States with high Latino populations, such as California, Texas, Florida, Arizona, and New Mexico, have voter participation marked by the growing influence of Latino voters. These states tend to have greater diversity in their voting patterns, with Latinos historically leaning toward the Democratic Party, although some subgroups, such as Cuban-Americans in Florida, support the Republican Party.

- In states like Georgia and Michigan, where there are large African American populations, the participation of this group is key to overall electoral victories.

49

b. Socioeconomic level and education

Voters with higher levels of education and better incomes tend to participate in elections in greater numbers. In states like Colorado and Massachusetts, where the educational level is higher compared to the national average, voter turnout is usually high, and voters tend to lean toward the Democratic Party.

On the other hand, in states with lower socioeconomic levels, such as Mississippi or Alabama, voter participation tends to be lower, especially among the most disadvantaged communities.

c. Voting policies and accessibility

Each state's voting laws and policies play a crucial role in determining voter turnout. Some states have laws that make voting more accessible, such as automatic voter registration, early voting, and mail-in voting. Other states have stricter laws to ensure electoral transparency, such as photo identification requirements or limitations on early voting, which may deter some groups from voting.

- California and Oregon are examples of liberal states with highly accessible voting policies, including widespread mail-in voting and automatic registration. This has led to higher voter turnout in these states, but also to more complaints about a lack of electoral transparency and reports of non-citizens voting, which is illegal in federal and state elections in the United States.
- In contrast, more conservative states like Texas and Florida have implemented stricter laws to ensure the integrity of electoral processes and voting accessibility for those legally eligible to vote.

Voting trends by state

a. Democratic States (Blue States)

Blue states are those that consistently vote for the Democratic Party in presidential and legislative elections. These states are usually located on the east and west coasts of the country and tend to have urban and diverse populations, as well as higher educational levels.

- California, New York, Massachusetts, and Illinois are examples of solidly Democratic states. In these states, voters tend to support liberal policies on issues like climate change, education, healthcare, and civil rights. The large cities in these states, such as Los Angeles, New York, and Chicago, also tend to have young and diverse populations, which reinforces the preference for Democrats.

- In addition, blue states often have a strong union presence, which also influences support for Democrats.

b. Republican States (Red States)

Red states are those that consistently vote for the Republican Party in elections. Some of these states are located in the south and center of the country.

Texas, Florida, Alabama, Oklahoma, Kentucky, and Wyoming are examples of solidly Republican states. Voters in these states tend to support conservative policies on issues such as taxes, business regulation, gun control, and traditional social values.

Red states tend to have a strong religious influence, particularly evangelical Christianity, which drives conservative social policy.

c. Purple States (Battleground States)

Purple states, also known as battleground states, are those where the vote can swing between the two main parties in each election. These states are crucial in presidential elections because they can determine the final outcome in the Electoral College. Voting trends in these states vary widely from one election to another and depend heavily on voter mobilization and circumstantial factors, such as the economy or candidates.

- Pennsylvania, Wisconsin, Michigan, Arizona, and Georgia are examples of battleground states. In the 2020 presidential election, these states were key to Joe Biden's victory, especially in places like Arizona and Georgia, which turned from red to blue for the first time in several decades. In these states, urban areas tend to vote for Democrats, while rural areas support Republicans.

d. States in transition

Some states that have traditionally been Republican or Democratic are showing signs of change due to factors such as demographic growth, internal migration, and changes in political priorities.

- Texas, traditionally a red state, is beginning to show signs of transitioning to a more competitive state due to the rapid growth of Latino and young populations in cities like Houston, Dallas, and Austin. Although it remains predominantly Republican, the margin of victory has narrowed in recent elections.
- Georgia, a historically Republican state, turned blue in the 2020 presidential election, in part due to the mobilization of African American and Latino voters in the Atlanta area.

Cultural differences and key issues in participation and voting trends

a. Immigration and cultural diversity issues

States with greater ethnic diversity, such as California, Florida, and Arizona, tend to place more importance on immigration policies and minority rights. In these states, immigration is a key issue that mobilizes both Latino and Asian-American voters.

b. Economy and employment

In states with economies more based on manufacturing and energy, such as Michigan, Ohio, Texas, and Pennsylvania, voters tend to focus on economic and employment policies. In these states, the economy plays a decisive role in elections, and Republicans tend to have more support in rural and manufacturing areas, while Democrats find backing in urban and industrial areas.

c. Social values and religion

In states with a strong religious influence, such as Alabama, Mississippi, and Texas, social policies, such as abortion rights and same-sex marriage, tend to mobilize more conservative voters. These states usually support Republicans due to their stance in defense of traditional values.

Florida as an example of political transition

In recent decades, Florida has been considered a battleground or purple state, alternating its support between the Democratic Party and the Republican Party in presidential and state elections. However, in recent years, Florida has shown a more pronounced trend toward the Republican

Party, especially after the 2020 presidential election and the 2022 midterm elections. This shift toward conservatism has led many analysts to consider Florida a red state today.

What happened?
The role of conservative latino voters

One of the main reasons for Florida's shift toward a more Republican state is the growth and mobilization of conservative-leaning Latino voters, particularly in South Florida.

a. The influence of cuban-americans

Cuban-Americans have historically been a key group of conservative voters in Florida. Due to their experience as exiles from FIDEL CASTRO'S communist regime, many Cubans in the United States, especially in Miami-Dade County, have consistently supported the Republican Party due to its hardline stance against authoritarian regimes in Cuba and Latin America. The Republican Party's firm foreign policy toward Cuba has been a key factor in maintaining Cuban-American support.

b. The growing Venezuelan and Nicaraguan population

In addition to Cuban-Americans, Venezuelan and Nicaraguan immigrants have grown in number in Florida, particularly after the political and economic crises in their home countries. Many of these immigrants align with the conservative values of the Republican Party due to their own experiences with left-wing authoritarian regimes, such as NICOLÁS MADURO in Venezuela and DANIEL ORTEGA in Nicaragua.

This voting bloc has been key to the Republican Party reinforcing its presence in Florida, as both Cuban-Americans and Venezuelans and Nicaraguans support anti-communist policies and strong sanctions against these regimes.

c. Effective republican mobilization among latinos

The Republican Party has been particularly effective in courting Latino voters in Florida, using campaigns that highlight key issues such as economic freedom, anti-communism, and conservative family values. Through messaging that links left-wing politics to the negative experiences of voters in their home countries, Republicans have managed to consolidate a strong base among Latinos in South Florida.

The increase in the retired conservative population

Florida has been a popular retirement destination for decades due to its warm climate and favorable tax policies (there is no state income tax). In recent years, there has been a significant influx of retirees moving to Florida from more liberal states like New York, Illinois, and California.

This population tends to lean toward the Republican Party due to their concerns about issues like taxes, government regulation, the economy, and security. Retirees moving to communities like The Villages and other areas of central and northern Florida have contributed to making these regions Republican strongholds.

Ron DeSantis' policies and his popularity among conservatives

Florida Governor Ron DeSantis has been a key figure in the state's political transformation toward a more conservative inclination. Since taking office in 2019, DeSantis has implemented policies that have resonated deeply with the Republican base, including:

- **COVID-19 Pandemic Management**: DeSantis gained popularity among conservatives for his approach to keeping Florida open for much of the COVID-19 pandemic, in contrast to other states that imposed stricter restrictions. His stance on personal freedom and the economy was well received by many Democratic, Republican, and independent voters.

- **Education policies**: DeSantis has promoted conservative policies in education, such as banning the teaching of critical race theory in public schools and protecting parental rights in educational decisions, policies that have attracted conservative voters.

- **Gun rights and public safety**: DeSantis has defended Second Amendment rights and promoted policies that strengthen public safety, such as protecting police officers and increasing penalties for violent protesters.

His conservative leadership has consolidated support among Republican voters and projected him as a figure of national importance within the party.

Chapter 2

Internal migration and demographic changes

Florida's population growth has been driven in part by internal migration from more liberal states like California and New York, whose residents have moved to the state in search of better economic opportunities and more security and quality of life. Also, many of these internal migrants come from more conservative or rural states and have brought their Republican political inclinations with them.

The influx of these new residents has helped strengthen support for the Republican Party, especially in regions outside the urban centers of Miami and Orlando.

Democratic weakness in voter mobilization

Although Florida has traditionally been a battleground state, the Democratic Party has struggled to mobilize its voters in recent elections, leading to a decline in its influence in the state. Political scandals, lack of leadership, disconnection from Latino voters, and an extremely liberal agenda are just some of the causes of the Democratic Party's downfall in Florida.

a. Lack of mobilization in latino communities

Despite the large Puerto Rican and Central American population in Florida, the Democratic Party has struggled to effectively mobilize these communities compared to the Republican Party's success in attracting Cuban-American and Venezuelan voters. Democrats have not been able to translate the growth of these populations into a larger number of voters at the polls, weakening their position in key elections.

b. Decline in urban counties

The Democratic Party has lost ground in important strongholds like Miami-Dade County (with nearly 70% of the population being Latino), which used to be a reliable Democratic stronghold. In the 2020 elections, DONALD TRUMP improved his performance in Miami-Dade compared to the 2016 elections, and in 2022 Governor DESANTIS won the county amid a "red wave" that changed the state.

Shifts in the political preferences of the working class

Florida has seen a shift in the political preferences of the white and Latino working class, which previously supported the Democratic Party but has in recent years shown a growing inclination toward the Republican Party, attracted by former President DONALD TRUMP'S rhetoric and economic policies focused on tax cuts and deregulation. These voters see the Republican Party as a defense of workers' interests against what they perceive as a socialist political and economic elite.

Expansion of the latino vote in non-traditionally latino states: Georgia, North Carolina, and Nevada

The growth of the Latino population in the United States has transformed the electoral landscape in several states, including those that historically did not have large Latino communities. States like Georgia, North Carolina, and Nevada have experienced a significant increase in the number of Latino residents, leading to an expansion of the Latino vote in these places. This trend has notably influenced state and federal elections, transforming some of these states into competitive battlegrounds where the Latino vote is increasingly crucial.

Georgia: The rapid growth of the latino vote in the southeast

Growth of the latino population

In recent decades, Georgia has experienced one of the fastest-growing Latino populations in the entire United States. From having a relatively small Latino population 30 years ago, Georgia has seen more than a 300 % increase in its Latino population since 1990. Currently, there are approximately 1.1 million Latinos living in Georgia, representing 11 % of the state's total population.

Geographic distribution

Most of the Latino population in Georgia is concentrated in the Atlanta metropolitan area, particularly in Gwinnett, Cobb, Fulton, and DeKalb counties. However, there is a growing Latino presence in more suburban and rural areas, such as southern Georgia and areas near industrial and agricultural centers.

Political impact

The growth of the Latino population has had a profound impact on Georgia's politics, especially in the 2020 presidential election, when the state turned Democratic for the first time since 1992. The Latino vote was a decisive factor in JOE BIDEN's victory in Georgia, as the Latino community, along with African Americans and young voters, drove voter turnout in key areas like the Atlanta metropolitan area.

In the 2021 Georgia Senate elections, Latino voters also played a fundamental role in the victories of JON OSSOFF and RAPHAEL WARNOCK, which allowed Democrats to take control of the U.S. Senate.

Mobilization factors

The mobilization of Latino voters in Georgia has been largely driven by grassroots organizations focused on registering new Latino voters, guiding them through the electoral process, and mobilizing them to vote. Groups affiliated with the Democratic Party, such as GALEO (Georgia Association of Latino Elected Officials) and Mi Familia Vota, are responsible for mobilizing part of the Latino vote in the state.

The growth of the Latino population in Georgia is influenced by the expansion of economic sectors like construction, manufacturing, and services, which have attracted many Latino workers to suburban and rural areas of the state. The second generation of Latinos born in Georgia, who are now citizens eligible to vote, has also increased voter participation.

Voting trends

Latino voters in Georgia tend to overwhelmingly support the Democratic Party, especially on issues such as immigration, healthcare access, and civil rights. However, there are more conservative sectors within the Latino community, particularly those who value economic security and traditional social values.

North Carolina: A transition state with a growing latino population

Growth of the latino population

Like Georgia, North Carolina has seen a rapid increase in its Latino population in recent decades. The Latino population has grown by 400 %

since 1990, and today there are more than 1 million Latinos in the state, representing about 10 % of North Carolina's total population.

Geographic distribution

The Latino population in North Carolina is widely dispersed, with large concentrations in the Charlotte, Raleigh-Durham metropolitan area, and in the agricultural and rural areas of the state, especially in eastern and central North Carolina, where many Latinos work in agriculture, construction, and service industries.

Political impact

TThe growing number of Latino voters has begun to have a significant impact on North Carolina's politics, a historically competitive state that has fluctuated between Democrats and Republicans in recent presidential elections. In 2020, the state voted for former Republican President Donald Trump, and the Latino vote was key in that victory in several urban areas.

At the local and state levels, Latinos are gaining influence, especially in urban and suburban areas where their presence has grown rapidly. In cities like Charlotte, the mobilization of Latino voters is beginning to affect municipal and state elections, tipping some contests toward the Democratic Party and others toward the Republican Party.

Mobilization factors

In North Carolina, community organizations have been crucial in mobilizing Latino voters. Groups like El Pueblo, a liberal Latino advocacy organization, and NC Latino Power have worked to register Latino voters.

The second generation of Latinos in North Carolina is also playing an important role, as many young people born in the state are reaching voting age and getting involved in political activism, both locally and statewide.

Voting trends

Latino voters in North Carolina tend to overwhelmingly support the Democratic Party, although there are conservative sectors that have supported the Republican Party, especially in rural areas where Latinos work in industries such as agriculture. Immigration policies, labor rights, and healthcare access are key issues for Latino voters in this state.

Nevada: The latino vote transforming a purple state

Growth of the latino population

Nevada is another state that has experienced rapid growth in its Latino population, particularly in the last decade. Currently, Latinos constitute about 30 % of the state's total population, with more than 800,000 Latino residents in Nevada, a significant portion of whom are eligible to vote.

Geographic distribution

Most of the Latino population in Nevada is concentrated in the Las Vegas metropolitan area and Clark County, although there are also Latino communities in Reno and other rural areas of the state. Many Latinos in Nevada work in the tourism and service industries, particularly in the casinos and hotels of Las Vegas.

Political impact

The Latino vote was decisive in Nevada in the 2020 presidential election. JOE BIDEN won the state largely thanks to the support of Latino voters in Clark County, where Las Vegas is located. In fact, Latinos have played a crucial role in making Nevada a purple state.

Nevada is a key state in presidential elections due to its position as one of the swing states. Latino voters have been fundamental to Democratic and Republican victories in recent elections, and their participation is seen as crucial for local and state contests, such as gubernatorial elections and the U.S. Senate.

Mobilization factors

The mobilization of Latino voters in Nevada has been driven by liberal organizations such as Mi Familia Vota and Battle Born Progress, which have worked to register new Latino voters and increase voter turnout in local and national elections. In addition, unions have played an important role in mobilizing Latino voters, especially in the hotel and casino industry.

Union activism, particularly through the Culinary Workers Union, has been key in mobilizing Latino workers in Las Vegas, many of whom work in the hospitality industry and have strong political participation through their unions.

Voting trends

Latino voters in Nevada have overwhelmingly supported the Democratic Party in the last 2020 elections due to issues such as immigration, labor rights, and healthcare access. However, there is a growing number of Latino voters who support the Republican Party, especially in rural areas and among Latinos of Cuban and South American origin, who tend to be more conservative.

Pennsylvania: The crown jewel of swing states?

The latino vote in Pennsylvania: Importance and analysis

Pennsylvania is one of the key states in U.S. presidential elections due to its weight in the Electoral College and its status as a battleground state. In recent elections, the Latino vote has gained more importance in this state, as their participation has been decisive in tight contests. Although the Latino community in Pennsylvania is not as large as in California or Texas, its growth and mobilization have made Latino voters a key group in state and federal elections.

Latino population in Pennsylvania

Where are they and how many are there?

Currently, the Latino population in Pennsylvania exceeds 1 million people, representing about 8 % of the state's total population. Although this percentage is smaller than in other states with large Latino populations, the Latino community in Pennsylvania has grown considerably in recent decades.

In terms of voters, it is estimated that there are around 500,000 Latinos eligible to vote in Pennsylvania. However, one of the challenges has been mobilizing this population to exercise their right to vote in greater numbers, something that has improved in the 2020-2022 electoral cycles.

The majority of Latinos in Pennsylvania are of Puerto Rican origin, as this state has been a popular destination for Puerto Ricans moving from the island or other parts of the northeast, such as New York and New Jersey. The migration of Puerto Ricans to Pennsylvania accelerated after Hurricane Maria hit the island in 2017 –one of the most devastating weather events in Puerto Rico's recent history– when many Puerto Ricans moved to the state in search of better economic opportunities and social stability.

In addition to Puerto Ricans, there is also a significant presence of Latinos of Mexican, Dominican, and other Central and South American origins, particularly in urban areas.

Geographic distribution of the latino vote in Pennsylvania

The Latino population is primarily concentrated in the urban and suburban areas of Pennsylvania, such as:

- **Philadelphia**: Philadelphia is home to the largest concentration of Latinos in the state. Here, the Puerto Rican community is particularly strong, and the Latino vote has been key in tilting elections in the city.
- **Lehigh Valley**: Cities like Allentown and Bethlehem have important Latino communities, including many Puerto Ricans and Dominicans. The Lehigh Valley has experienced steady growth in its Latino population, increasing the importance of the vote in this region.
- **Reading**: Another city with a large Latino population, where Puerto Ricans and Dominicans make up an important part of the community.
- **Lancaster and Harrisburg**: TThese areas have also seen an increase in the Latino population in recent years.

The Weight of the latino vote in Pennsylvania

Can it define a presidential election?

Yes, the Latino vote can define a presidential election in Pennsylvania. Since the state is one of the most important battlegrounds in presidential elections, any increase in participation by key groups, such as Latino voters, can be decisive. In 2020, JOE BIDEN won Pennsylvania by a narrow margin of about 80,000 votes, and the Latino vote was crucial in areas like Philadelphia and Allentown.

In a state where elections are usually close, an increase in Latino participation has the potential to tip the balance toward one party or the other. As the Latino community grows and becomes more effectively mobilized, its impact on presidential, legislative, and local elections in Pennsylvania will only continue to grow.

Voting trends of latino voters in Pennsylvania

Support for the democratic party

Historically, Latinos in Pennsylvania have shown strong preference for the Democratic Party. Latino voters, especially Puerto Ricans, have been a reliable base for Democrats in Philadelphia and other urban areas of the state.

Growth of the republican vote among latinos

Although Democrats have dominated the Latino vote in Pennsylvania, there are indications of a growing group of Latino voters leaning toward the Republican Party, particularly in rural areas or among more conservative Latinos. This segment of voters tends to be concerned about issues such as the economy, taxes, and conservative family values.

Overall, however, Latinos in Pennsylvania remain a solid base for the Democratic Party (2020), especially in the larger cities.

Factors driving latino voter mobilization in Pennsylvania

Several factors have contributed to the increase in Latino voter mobilization and participation in Pennsylvania:

- **Community organization**: Organizations affiliated with the Democratic Party and ultra-liberal groups like "Make the Road Pennsylvania" work specifically to register Latino voters.

- **Immigration and civil rights policies**: Latinos in Pennsylvania, like those in other parts of the country, are particularly concerned about issues such as immigration, healthcare access, and civil rights. These concerns have led to increased participation by Latino voters.

- **Growth of the second generation**: As more U.S.-born Latinos reach voting age, the base of Latino voters in Pennsylvania has grown considerably. This second generation of Latinos tends to be more politically engaged and more likely to vote than their immigrant parents.

History *of the* latino vote *in the* United States

The Latino vote in the United States has gained increasing relevance in presidential and midterm elections since the late 20th century. As the Latino population has grown, so has their political participation, making them a key voting bloc. However, as we have explained, Latino voting behavior is not monolithic, as it varies by region, country of origin, age, and the key issues of each election.

The evolution of the latino vote (1998-2023)

1998-2000: Early signs of latino vote growth

By the late 1990s, the Latino population in the United States was growing rapidly due to immigration and birth rates, but their electoral participation was still below that of other demographic groups. In the 2000 presidential election, it was estimated that about 5.9 million Latinos voted, representing 5.4 % of the electorate.

In this election, Latinos nationally favored AL GORE with the popular vote (62 %) over GEORGE W. BUSH (35 %), but participation was limited. Regionally, support for Democrats was stronger in states like California, while Republicans found more backing in Texas and Florida.

This historic 2000 election, between Democrat AL GORE and Republican GEORGE W. BUSH, was decided in Florida by an extremely small margin of 537 votes. After weeks of recounts and legal disputes, the final decision was left to the U.S. Supreme Court, which ended the recount in Florida in the case BUSH v. GORE. This allowed Bush to win the state's 25 electoral votes, securing his victory in the Electoral College.

The Latino vote in Florida, mainly Cuban-American, gave President BUSH the victory, setting a precedent for the power of the Hispanic vote in the United States.

2004 Presidential Election: Consolidation of the latino vote

In 2004, Latino participation increased significantly, reaching approximately 7.6 million Latino voters, representing 6 % of the electorate. The election between GEORGE W. BUSH and JOHN KERRY marked an important point, as BUSH managed to capture 44% of the Latino vote, a significantly higher percentage than in previous elections, thanks to his focus on education, immigration, and his popularity among Latino voters in Texas and Florida.

However, JOHN KERRY won the majority of the Latino vote (53 %), especially in states like California and New York, where concerns about the Iraq War and immigrant rights were key issues.

2006 Midterm Elections: Immigration as a central issue

The 2006 midterm elections were marked by the debate over immigration reform and immigration policies. In this context, Latinos mobilized in greater numbers to support Democrats, who won control of Congress. Democrats received overwhelming support from 69 % of the Latino vote, partly due to the perception that the Republican Party had a more restrictive stance on immigration.

2008 Presidential Election: The OBAMA era

The election of BARACK OBAMA in 2008 marked a turning point in the history of the Latino vote in the United States. In this election, Latinos played a crucial role in securing OBAMA'S victory, particularly in key states like Nevada, Colorado, New Mexico, and Florida.

Participation and mobilization

In 2008, 9.7 million Latinos voted, representing approximately 7.4 % of the electorate. This was a record number of participation at the time, and the result of a strong campaign to mobilize Latino voters by OBAMA'S team. Community organizations, unions, and civil rights groups worked together to increase the registration and participation of Latino voters, especially in urban and suburban areas where the Latino community was growing rapidly.

Key issues for latinos

Latinos supported OBAMA because of his focus on issues critical to the community, such as:

- **Immigration reform:** OBAMA promised comprehensive immigration reform, including a path to citizenship for undocumented immigrants. Although the reform did not materialize during his first term, the promise to address the issue attracted many Latino voters.
- **Economy and jobs:** After the 2008 financial crisis, the economy was a priority issue, and Latinos supported OBAMA's proposal to stimulate the economy and protect jobs.
- **Healthcare:** OBAMA made affordable healthcare a priority, which resonated with the Latino community, which often faces difficulties accessing health services.

Results

OBAMA won 67 % of the Latino vote, while his Republican opponent, JOHN MCCAIN, captured 31 %. This strong Latino support was decisive in several key states. In Nevada, for example, OBAMA obtained 76 % of the Latino vote, contributing to his comfortable victory in the state. In Colorado, he won 61 % of the Latino vote, helping him win the state, which had been Republican in the 2004 elections. New Mexico, a state with a significant Latino population, was also won by OBAMA with 69 % of the Latino vote.

In summary, the Latino vote in 2008 was key to securing OBAMA's victory in several battleground states. This election also marked the beginning of a trend in which Democrats managed to capture a solid majority of the Latino vote in presidential elections.

2010 Midterm Elections: Challenges for democrats

In 2010, during the midterm elections, Democrats suffered major losses in Congress, but the Latino vote remained loyal to the party. Latinos voted 60 % for Democrats, although there was some disillusionment due to the lack of progress on immigration reform. Republicans managed to capture 38 % of the Latino vote, particularly among more conservative voters in states like Florida and Texas.

2012 Presidential Election: The Re-election of Barack H. Obama

In 2012, Barack Obama was re-elected with strong support from the Latino community, which represented approximately 10 % of the electorate, with 11.2 million Latinos voting. Obama won 71 % of the Latino vote, compared to 27 % for Mitt Romney.

Key issues for latinos

In 2012, several issues were particularly important for Latino voters:

- **Deferred Action for Childhood Arrivals (DACA):** Obama implemented the DACA program in 2012, which protected young undocumented immigrants from deportation. This was seen as a crucial measure by the Latino community, which largely supported the creation of this program.
- **Economy:** Although the economy remained a major concern, the unemployment rate was decreasing, and Obama's administration had begun to see positive results in economic recovery.
- **Healthcare:** The Affordable Care Act (ACA) was viewed favorably by Latinos, as many benefited from access to affordable health insurance under this law.

Results

Latinos were decisive in states like Nevada, where Obama won 71 % of the Latino vote, and Colorado, where he obtained 75 % of the Latino vote, securing his victory in these key states. Additionally, in Florida, Obama won 60 % of the Latino vote, helping him win this crucial battleground state.

2014 Midterm Elections: Low latino participation

In the 2014 midterm elections, Latino voter turnout was low compared to the presidential elections. Only 6.8 million Latinos voted, representing a significant drop in participation. Republicans managed to capture around 36 % of the Latino vote, while Democrats maintained 62 %.

This low turnout affected Democrats, who lost control of the Senate. The lack of progress on immigration reform and disappointment with Obama's policies contributed to Latino voter apathy in this election.

Chapter 3

2016 Presidential Election: The impact of TRUMP

In 2016, DONALD TRUMP won the presidency with a new record! Some 12.7 million Latinos voted, representing 11.9 % of the electorate. TRUMP captured around 30% of the Latino vote, a considerably high percentage for a Republican candidate.

- **Cuban-Americans** in Florida mostly voted for TRUMP, favoring his firm stance against the Cuban regime and his hardline foreign policy toward Venezuela and other socialist regimes in Latin America.
- **Conservative and evangelical Latinos** in states like Texas and Arizona also voted for TRUMP, attracted by his proposals in favor of economic freedom, tax cuts, and conservative values.

However, Democratic candidate HILLARY CLINTON won approximately 60 % of the Latino vote, although not with the same strength as BARACK OBAMA in previous elections. She failed to mobilize enough Latino voters in states like Florida and Texas, while Trump in Florida won a majority share of the Cuban-American vote, which helped him win the Sunshine State. In Nevada and Colorado, CLINTON won with Latino support, but it was not enough to secure her a national victory.

2018 Midterm Elections

In 2018, approximately 11.7 million Latinos voted, a record number for a midterm election. Democrats won 69 % of the Latino vote, while Republicans obtained 29 %.

Issues such as immigration, healthcare, and gun control mobilized Latino voters, helping Democrats regain control of the House of Representatives.

2020 Presidential Election: Record participation

In 2020, the Latino vote was once again decisive in JOE BIDEN's victory over DONALD TRUMP. This election saw a record Latino turnout and a greater focus on mobilization efforts in key states.

In 2020, Latinos represented approximately 13.3 % of the electorate, with a record 16.6 million Latinos voting. JOE BIDEN won 65 % of the Latino vote, while DONALD TRUMP achieved his best performance with 32 % of the

Latino vote, one of the highest proportions for a Republican candidate in decades. Although BIDEN dominated the Latino vote in states like Nevada and Arizona, TRUMP improved his performance in Florida and Texas, where he captured a significant portion of the Cuban-American vote and conservative Latinos in border areas.

This increase in Latino support for Trump surprised many analysts and was due to several factors.

- **Conservative and religious latinos:** TRUMP gained ground among conservative Latinos, especially evangelicals and practicing Catholics, who supported his positions on abortion and traditional family values.
- **Growing support in Florida and Texas:** TRUMP achieved impressive results in Florida, where he won more than 45 % of the Latino vote, driven by strong support from Cuban-Americans and Venezuelans in South Florida. In Texas, he also improved his performance in traditionally Democratic areas in the south of the state, capturing a significant share of the Latino vote, particularly among Tejanos in rural and border areas.
- **Economy and jobs:** Many latinos appreciated TRUMP'S work on economic freedom and job creation.

The Latino vote was crucial in states like Arizona, Nevada, and Pennsylvania, where BIDEN'S victory margins were narrow, and Latino support was decisive in giving him the presidency.

2022 Midterm Elections: Increasing diversification of the latino vote

In the 2022 midterm elections, Latinos continued to play a key role. Although the majority of Latinos voted for Democrats, there was increasing diversity in Latino voting behavior, with a higher percentage supporting Republicans. This reaffirms the Latino vote as a dynamic and decisive group, especially in key states.

General figures

- According to data from NALEO (National Association of Latino Elected and Appointed Officials), about 11.6 million Latinos voted in the 2022 elections, representing significant participation, although slightly lower than in the 2020 presidential elections.

- Latinos constituted approximately 10% of the total electorate in the 2022 elections, a relevant electoral bloc in deciding key contests in states like Arizona, Nevada, Georgia, and Texas.

State results

- **Florida:** In this state, Governor RON DESANTIS and Senator MARCO RUBIO, both Republicans, achieved significant victories driven in part by strong support from Latino voters, particularly Cuban-Americans and Venezuelans. In Miami-Dade County, DESANTIS won by a wide margin, reflecting a notable shift towards Republicans compared to previous elections.

- **Nevada:** Latino voters helped Democrats secure the victory of Senator CATHERINE CORTEZ MASTO in a tight race. Approximately 63 % of Latino voters supported Democrats in Nevada, according to exit polls.

- **Arizona:** Latinos played a crucial role in the election of Democrat Senator MARK KELLY and Democrat Governor KATIE HOBBS, in a historically Republican state.

Party preferences

- Nationally, 60 % of Latino voters supported Democrats in the 2022 elections, while approximately 39 % voted for Republican candidates, reflecting a reduced margin of support for Democrats compared to previous elections.

- Republicans increased their support among Latinos, where issues such as the economy, border control, and social conservatism resonated with certain segments of the Latino community.

Key issues for latinos

- **Economy:** Inflation and the cost of living were the most important issues for Latino voters, influencing their decision to support both Republicans and Democrats in different states.

- **Inmigración:** Although immigration remains a key issue, other issues such as the economy, healthcare, and education were more decisive in Latino voters' decisions in 2022.

Emerging trends: Young latino voters and changes in participation among different latino subgroups

As we have seen, the Latino community in the United States is far from being a homogeneous group, and emerging trends in their voting behavior reflect this diversity. In recent years, young Latino voters have gained prominence in U.S. politics, driving significant changes in participation and political preferences. At the same time, different subgroups within the Latino community, such as Mexicans, Cubans, Puerto Ricans, Venezuelans, and Central Americans, have shown variations in their voting behavior, transforming the political landscape in key states.

This analysis delves into the emerging trends among young Latino voters and how the different Latino communities have influenced and will continue to influence U.S. politics.

The rise of young latino voters: The generation defining the future

Demographics and growth of young latinos

Young Latinos are emerging as a crucial demographic group in the United States. With a median age of 29, compared to the general U.S. population's 38 years, Latinos are a young community. Of the 62 million Latinos living in the United States, about 16 million are between the ages of 18 and 35. This youth means that Latinos have enormous potential for electoral influence in the coming decades.

Each year, nearly 1 million young Latinos reach voting age, constantly increasing the size of the Latino electorate. By 2030, Latinos are expected to make up 18 % of the national electorate, driven largely by this youthful growth.

Election participation

Although historically, Latino voters, and especially young Latino voters, have had lower turnout rates than other groups, this trend has begun to change. In the 2020 presidential election, young Latino turnout reached record levels, with a significant increase in voter mobilization among those aged 18 to 29.

This increase in participation was partly driven by activism around key issues such as social justice, immigration, climate change, and access to education and healthcare. Community groups and NGOs have played a central role in mobilizing young Latino voters, using social media, digital campaigns, and community activism to register new voters and get them to the polls.

Key issues for young latinos

Young Latino voters tend to be more aligned with liberal positions compared to older generations. The issues that most mobilize young Latinos include:

- **Social and racial justice:** Young Latinos have been an important part of the racial justice movement in the United States, participating in protests and social activism.

- **Immigration:** Immigration remains a priority issue for many young Latinos, especially those who are children of immigrants or DACA recipients. Defending immigrant rights and ending restrictive policies are central issues.

- **Climate change:** Young Latinos are also concerned about the impact of climate change, as many Latino communities are disproportionately affected by pollution and limited access to natural resources.

- **Healthcare access:** Access to healthcare is another critical issue, as healthcare disparities continue to affect the Latino community.

These concerns are leading young Latinos to vote in greater numbers and to largely support Democratic Party candidates, although some more conservative groups, especially religious Latinos, have shown support for the Republican Party.

Changes in Participation Among Different Latino Subgroups

Despite their shared identification as Latinos, different subgroups within the Latino community have shown variations in their participation patterns and voting behavior. These differences reflect diverse immigration experiences, economic realities, and the influence of U.S. foreign policy on their countries of origin. Below are the emerging trends among the largest Latino subgroups in the United States:

73

a. Mexicans: The largest and most diverse latino group

Demographics

Mexicans are the largest Latino group in the United States, representing more than 60 % of the total Latino population. They are concentrated primarily in states like California, Texas, Arizona, New Mexico, and Illinois, but their presence is growing in other regions, including parts of the Northeast and the Sout.

Electoral participation

Mexican voter participation has steadily increased, especially since the 1990s. In the 2020 elections, Mexicans represented the majority of Latino voters in key states like California and Texas.

While they have historically voted overwhelmingly for the Democratic Party, especially on issues such as immigration, healthcare, and civil rights, there has been a notable shift of some Mexican voters toward the Republican Party, particularly in Texas border areas like the Rio Grande Valley, where Republicans made significant gains in 2020.

Emerging trends

- **Young mexicans:** Similar to other young Latinos, young Mexican voters tend to support progressive policies and are increasingly mobilized around issues of social justice, climate change, and economic equality.
- **Regional influences:** Mexican voters in Texas and other border states have shown a greater openness to Republican candidates due to concerns about security and employment in their communities.

b. Cubans: A conservative group in evolution

Demographics

Cubans have been a key Latino subgroup in U.S. politics, especially in Florida, where they represent an important electoral bloc. Unlike other Latino groups, Cubans have tended to vote predominantly for the Republican Party, largely due to their historical opposition to FIDEL CASTRO's communist regime and their support for hardline policies toward Cuba.

Electoral participation

Cubans have shown high levels of voter turnout compared to other Latino subgroups. In Florida, their influence has been key to tilting presidential elections in favor of Republicans, as was the case in 2016 and 2020, when DONALD TRUMP received strong Cuban-American support.

Emerging trends

- **Young generation and political change:** While the older generation of Cubans remains predominantly conservative, the younger generation of Cuban-Americans is showing a trend of moving away from Republican orthodoxy, more often supporting progressive issues like social justice and climate change. However, there remains a strong generational divide.

- **Growing diversity in Florida:** As the Venezuelan and Puerto Rican communities grow in Florida, Cubans are no longer the dominant Latino group, which could lead to a shift in the state's political trends in the future.

c. Puerto Ricans: A growing electoral power in the Northeast and Florida

Demographics

Puerto Ricans make up the second-largest Latino group in the United States, with a significant population in New York, New Jersey, Pennsylvania, and more recently in Florida.

Electoral participation

Since Puerto Ricans are U.S. citizens by birth, they have high potential for electoral participation. In Florida, Puerto Ricans have played an increasingly important role, tilting the Latino vote toward the Democratic Party, especially in areas like Orlando and central Florida.

Emerging trends

- **Impact of migration:** Puerto Ricans who moved to Florida after Hurricane Maria are increasingly involved in local and national politics. Although they have historically supported Democrats, there is a growing number leaning toward Republicans, especially on economic and security issues.

- **Activism around Puerto Rico:** Many Puerto Ricans are mobilized around issues related to the island's political status and debt relief; topics that continue to be central to their political participation.

d. Venezuelans: An emerging group with conservative leanings

Demographics

Venezuelan migration to the United States has grown significantly in the past decade due to the political and economic crisis in Venezuela. Most Venezuelans in the United States are concentrated in Florida, although their presence is increasing in Texas, New York, New Jersey, and Washington, D.C.

Electoral participation

Venezuelan voters, many of whom have fled socialist regimes, tend to lean toward the Republican Party, supporting hardline policies against leftist governments in Latin America. In the 2020 elections, Venezuelans in Florida played an important role in Trump's victory in the state.

Emerging trends

- **Growing conservatism:** Venezuelans in Florida have shown a conservative inclination, similar to that of Cubans, due to their experience with the Chávez regime in Venezuela. They are likely to remain a key electoral group for Republicans in Florida due to their strong stance against socialism.

Other Latino communities, such as Colombians, Argentinians, or Hondurans, also contribute to the power of the Latino vote.

Colombians and Argentinians are concentrated in areas like Weston, Miami, and West Palm Beach in Florida, influencing local elections. In California and Texas, Salvadorans, Hondurans, and Guatemalans are key, concentrated in cities like Los Angeles and Houston, while Brazilians are growing in influence in states like Florida and Massachusetts. They range from independents to Democrats and Republicans.

Chapter 4

The *U.S. electoral system*

Origin of the U.S. electoral system and the electoral college

The U.S. electoral system, including the Electoral College, was created by the Founding Fathers during the Constitutional Convention of 1787 in Philadelphia. This mechanism was a compromise between various models proposed for the election of the president.

Why was the electoral college created?

The main goal of the Electoral College was to balance different interests and resolve tensions between large and small states, between those who wanted a president elected directly by the people and those who preferred the president to be chosen by Congress. The main reasons for its creation are:

1. **Distrust of direct democracy:** The Founding Fathers did not fully trust the idea of a direct democracy in which the president would be chosen by popular vote, fearing that the public would not have enough knowledge about the candidates and that large cities or larger states would dominate the elections. They wanted a system that would give a voice to both large and small states, balancing interests.

2. **Federalism:** The system reflects the principles of federalism, which gives power to both the federal government and the states. The Electoral College allows the states to have a key role in electing the president, preserving the autonomy of the states.

3. **Compromise between large and small states:** Smaller states feared being dominated by larger ones if the president were elected by popular vote. The Electoral College gave them a more equitable voice

by assigning electors based on the number of senators (each state has two) and representatives (based on population).

4. **Avoiding regional dominance:** The founders wanted to prevent a candidate from winning the presidency with the support of just one region of the country, ignoring the rest. By distributing votes across states, they ensured that a candidate needed broad support from different regions to win.

How does the electoral College Work?

Each state has a number of electors equal to its representation in Congress: two senators and a number of representatives based on the state's population.

There are 538 total electors, and to win the presidency, a candidate needs a majority of 270 electoral votes.

In most states, the candidate who wins the popular vote in that state takes all the state's electoral votes. Only Maine and Nebraska use a pro-portional system where they distribute some of their electoral votes based on the results in individual districts.

Difference between the popular vote and the Electoral College

The popular vote reflects the direct choice of citizens, while the Electoral College is the mechanism that actually decides who will be president. This has led to outcomes where a candidate can win the popular vote but lose the Electoral College, as happened in:

- 2000: AL GORE won the popular vote, but GEORGE W. BUSH won the Electoral College and the presidency.
- 2016: HILLARY CLINTON won the popular vote, but DONALD TRUMP won the Electoral College and, therefore, the presidency.

Impact of the latino vote on the Electoral College

The Latino vote has played a crucial role in several key states with a significant number of electoral votes. For example:

- **Florida:** The Latino vote has been decisive in recent elections. With 30 electoral votes, Florida is an essential state to win the presidency.
- **Nevada and Arizona:** In the 2020 elections, the Latino vote was crucial for Joe Biden's victories in these states, with 6 and 11 electoral votes, respectively.
- **Texas:** The Latino vote in Texas determines its 40 electoral votes.

What if no candidate reaches the majority of electoral votes? The contingent election

A contingent election is a special process in the U.S. electoral system that is activated when no presidential or vice-presidential candidate obtains the majority of Electoral College votes. In this case, the U.S. Constitution establishes a resolution mechanism where Congress plays a decisive role.

How is a contingent election resolved?

Election of the president

- If no presidential candidate secures the necessary 270 electoral votes, the election is decided in the House of Representatives.
- Each state has one vote, regardless of its size or population. The delegation from each state (its representatives) votes internally to decide which candidate to support. The candidate who wins the majority of the votes (at least 26 of the 50 states) becomes president.

Election of the vice president

- If no vice-presidential candidate obtains the majority of electoral votes, the election is decided in the Senate.
- In this case, each senator has one vote, and the candidate who receives the majority (at least 51 votes) becomes vice president.

Examples of contingent elections in U.S. history

- The first and most famous contingent election occurred in 1800 when THOMAS JEFFERSON and AARON BURR tied in the Electoral College. The House of Representatives resolved the election by choosing JEFFERSON as president.

- The second contingent election took place in 1824 when none of the four presidential candidates obtained a majority of the electoral votes. The House of Representatives chose JOHN QUINCY ADAMS as president, despite ANDREW JACKSON winning the popular vote.

The contingent election process is very rare, but it is provided for in the Constitution to ensure that a president and vice president can be chosen when the Electoral College fails to do so.

Reforms and controversies

Throughout history, there have been proposals to reform or abolish the Electoral College, as some argue that it does not adequately represent the popular vote and gives too much weight to small states or a few "battleground" states. Despite these debates, the system has persisted since its creation and remains a central feature of U.S. presidential elections.

The Conventions

Las convenciones políticas en Estados Unidos son eventos clave en el procPolitical conventions in the United States are key events in the electoral process where political parties –mainly Democratic and Republican– officially select their candidates for president and vice president. They also serve to define the party's platform and unify its members around a common message heading into the general election. Although the nomination of the candidate is usually decided before the convention, these events are an opportunity to celebrate that decision and officially launch the presidential campaign.

What are conventions for?

1. **Official nomination of the candidate:** The main function of the convention is to officially select the presidential candidate and their running mate for vice president.
2. **Party unity:** It is an event where the party shows unity and motivation. Candidates who participated in the primaries typically endorse the official nominee.
3. **Presentation of the party platform:** During the convention, delegates vote and adopt an official platform detailing the party's positions on

issues such as the economy, health care, education, and foreign policy.

4. **Public projection:** The convention is a political marketing tool broadcast in the media, allowing the party to present its candidate and message to millions of people.

How do they work?

1. **Election of delegates:** Throughout the primary and caucus cycle, parties select state delegates. These delegates represent the voters of their state and attend the convention to vote for the candidate they prefer.

2. **Voting at the convention:** Delegates vote for the presidential candidate. In most cases, the candidate who has won the majority of delegates in the primaries and caucuses secures the nomination.

3. **Presentations and speeches:** Conventions include speeches from prominent political figures who seek to motivate voters and project a message of party unity and strength.

4. **Announcement of the vice-presidential candidate:** During the convention, the presidential candidate announces their running mate.

here are they held and why?

Conventions are held in large cities capable of hosting tens of thousands of people. The choice of city typically considers the political importance of the region and its infrastructure to handle an event of such magnitude.

2024 Conventions

- **Democratic National Convention (DNC):** Held in Chicago, Illinois. Chicago was selected for its history of Democratic support and its logistical capacity for large events.

- **Republican National Convention (RNC):** Republicans chose Milwaukee, Wisconsin. Wisconsin is a crucial "battleground" state, and Republicans hope to attract votes from this region to tip the balance in their favor.

How much do they cost?

Organizing a national convention can cost between $50 million and $100 million. Expenses include renting stadiums or convention centers, security, logistics, accommodation for delegates, and media production. Much of the funding comes from private sponsors and the political party.

Attendance and mobilization

Conventions mobilize a large number of people:

- **Delegates:** Approximately 4,000 delegates for each party, who represent the results of state primaries.
- **Press:** Hundreds of national and international media outlets cover the event.
- **Supporters and activists:** Thousands of supporters and party members attend to support their candidate and participate in event activities.

Caucuses

Caucuses are a type of political meeting where registered members of a political party gather to discuss and decide whom they will support as their candidate in the U.S. presidential elections. Unlike primaries, where voters cast secret ballots to choose their preferred candidate, caucuses are public meetings where voters discuss and choose delegates who will support a particular candidate at the party's convention.

How do Caucuses work?

1. **Local meetings:** Caucuses usually start at the local level, where registered party voters meet in gyms, schools, churches, or community centers. In these meetings, attendees discuss the candidates, and a vote is held at the end.
2. **Public process:** Unlike secret voting, the caucus process is more transparent and may include the formation of physical support groups for different candidates.
3. **Selection of delegates:** The results of the caucuses determine how many delegates will support each candidate at the state or national convention of the party.

Differences between caucuses and primaries

- **Primaries:** State-run elections where voters cast secret ballots for their preferred candidate.
- **Caucuses:** Organized by political parties and involve meetings where delegates are publicly selected to support candidates.

Examples of states with caucuses

- **Iowa:** Famous for holding the first caucus in the presidential election cycle, making it a key state for gauging early candidate support.
- **Nevada:** Another important state that holds caucuses, where the Latino vote has had increasing influence.

What are caucuses for?

Caucuses are crucial for determining the level of support for candidates at the local and state levels. While less common than primaries, caucuses play an important role in selecting delegates who will ultimately help nominate a presidential candidate at the party conventions.

Primary elections

Primary elections in the United States are processes in which political parties select their candidates for general elections. These elections allow voters to choose who will represent their party in upcoming presidential, congressional, state, or local elections.

Types of primary elections

1. **Closed primaries:** Only voters registered with a specific political party can vote in that party's primary. States like Florida, Nevada, and Kentucky have closed primaries.
2. **Open primaries:** Allow any registered voter, regardless of party affiliation, to vote in any party's primary. However, voters can only choose one primary to participate in, either Democratic or Republican, but not both. Colorado, Texas, and Vermont are good examples of states with open primaries.
3. **Semi-open or semi-closed primaries:** In this system, independents (or unaffiliated voters) can choose which primary to participate in, while

party-affiliated voters can only vote in their own party's primary. Indiana is an example of semi-open primaries.

4. **Runoff primaries:** If no candidate obtains an absolute majority in the first round, a runoff is held between the two candidates with the most votes.

Purpose of primary elections

The main goal is to select the official party candidates who will compete in the general elections. Primaries are essential to the U.S. democracy, as they allow citizens to have a say in their parties' nomination process.

Examples:

- In presidential elections, parties hold state primaries to select delegates who support the candidates. These delegates then participate in the party's national convention, where the presidential candidate is officially chosen.
- For local, state, or congressional offices, primaries determine which party candidate will advance to the general election.

In general, primary elections vary by state, and different jurisdictions commonly have different rules on how the process is conducted and who can participate.

Independent (nonpartisan) voting in the United Statess

Independent voters are those who do not identify with either the Democratic or Republican parties and make up a significant part of the U.S. electorate. In 2023, the percentage of voters identifying as independent reached a record average of 43 % of the U.S. electorate. This percentage has steadily increased over the past decades, partly due to growing dissatisfaction with traditional parties and generational changes.

Where are independent voters located?

There are approximately 168 million registered voters in the United States, according to the Census Bureau.

In absolute numbers, there are approximately 35.3 million registered independent voters in states that allow voters to register without party affiliation. This represents about 28.5 % of the total number of registered voters in those states.

States with the highest concentration of independent voters in 2024 include:

- **California:** Over 4.8 million independent voters.
- **Florida:** Approximately 3.5 million.
- **Nueva York:** About 2.9 million.

Other states with high proportions of independents include Massachusetts, where by 2024, 60.17 % of registered voters are independent; Alaska, with 58.08 % of registered voters being independent; and Colorado, which identifies 45.99 % of voters as independent.

Thus, independent voting defines elections in the United States, particularly in electoral "swing states" or battlegrounds.

How do independent voters vote?

Historically, independent voters do not follow a fixed trend and are known for their flexibility in switching parties with each election. Although they are not committed to a specific party, they tend to lean toward one or the other depending on the issues and candidates in each election cycle. In close elections, like the 2020 presidential election, independent voters played a crucial role in determining the outcome in key states like Arizona, Michigan, and Pennsylvania.

The issues that typically influence independent voters the most are:

- **Economy:** Especially inflation, employment, and cost of living.
- **Health care:** Access to health care is a constant concern.
- **Governance:** Independents tend to prefer policies that promote accountability and transparency.

Why don't independent voters join parties?

Many voters identify as independent due to growing dissatisfaction with the two-party system. Instead of fully aligning with a party platform, independents prefer to vote for candidates based on specific issues. Additionally, younger voters, such as Generation Z and Millennials, are more likely to be independent because they view the current political system as polarized and divisive.

The importance of the independent latino vote

The independent Latino vote has gained increasing relevance in the U.S. political landscape.

This group has shown a tendency to decide between Democrats and Republicans depending on the local context and the candidates in each election cycle. In other words, independent Latino voters choose the candidate rather than necessarily the candidate's party, making them a key electoral group that can swing elections, especially in "battleground" states.

Electoral behavior

- **Flexibility:** Independent Latino voters tend to be more flexible and open to changing their vote based on the candidates and policies proposed, making them an unpredictable electoral bloc.
- **Partial alignment:** Although many independent Latinos vote similarly to Democrats on social and immigration issues, some support Republicans on economic and security issues.

Independent voting behavior in presidential elections

The independent Latino vote has been a decisive factor in several recent presidential elections. Since the margins of victory in some states are very narrow, independent Latinos have been key in tipping the outcome.

2016 Presidential Election

- In 2016, DONALD TRUMP managed to capture a larger share of the independent Latino vote than many expected. About 28 % of independent Latinos voted for TRUMP, mainly driven by his focus on the economy, while HILLARY CLINTON won 66% of the overall Latino vote.
- **Key states: :** EIn states like Florida and Texas, where independent Latinos make up a considerable portion of the electorate, their vote was crucial to TRUMP'S victory in those states.

2020 Presidential Election

- In 2020, JOE BIDEN won 65 % of the Latino vote, including a significant portion of independent Latinos. However, DONALD TRUMP improved his performance among independent Latinos compared to 2016, winning 32 % of the total Latino vote, a notable increase.

- **Key states:** The independent Latino vote was key in states like Arizona and Nevada, where BIDEN gained a small but significant edge thanks to support from moderate independent Latinos.

Independent voting behavior in state elections

Independent Latino voting behavior has also impacted gubernatorial elections, particularly in states with large Latino populations like California, Nevada, Arizona, and Florida.

California gubernatorial election (2021)

- In the 2021 recall election of Governor GAVIN NEWSOM, independent Latino voters played a crucial role in defeating the recall attempt. Although many Latinos were initially undecided, NEWSOM'S campaign managed to capture their support by focusing on issues like healthcare access and immigration policies.

Florida gubernatorial elections

- In Florida, independent Latino voters have been more receptive to Republicans. RON DESANTIS, the current governor, captured a considerable share of the independent Latino vote in the 2018 election thanks to his focus on the economy and public safety. This support was key to his victory.

Independent voting behavior in congressional elections

Independent Latino voting behavior has been decisive in competitive congressional districts, especially in states like Texas, Nevada, and Florida, where the Latino vote represents a significant portion of the electorate.

Texas

- In the 2022 midterm elections, independent Latino voters were crucial in the election of MAYRA FLORES to Congress. Flores, a Republican, won in South Texas, a border region with a large Latino population, due to her stance on border security and conservative values. Her victory reflected growing support among independent Latino voters for Republican candidates in border districts.

Issues that drive independent latino voting

Independent Latino voters are not tied to a single party, and their electoral behavior is more influenced by the key issues of each election than by party loyalty. Among the issues that mobilize independent Latinos are:

Economy

- **Employment and economic growth:** For many independent Latinos, the economy is the most important issue. They prefer candidates who promote job creation, lower taxes, and offer incentives for small businesses. Republican economic policies have resonated with this group.

Health care and education

- Access to health care and improving the education system are top priorities for independent Latinos. Those who voted for Democrats in 2020 did so, in part, because Joe Biden promised to expand healthcare access and reduce healthcare costs.

Immigration

- Immigration remains a fundamental issue for Latinos, although independent Latino voters tend to have more moderate views. While some support comprehensive immigration reform, others back increased border security and measures to control illegal immigration.

Security and crime

- In some areas, especially border regions, concerns about security and crime have pushed independent Latino voters toward Republican candidates who advocate tough-on-crime policies and more resources for law enforcement.

Conservative values

- Independent Latinos with more religious or conservative inclinations regarding family values and abortion tend to favor Republican candidates, who often promote these values in their campaigns.

Religion and the Latino Vote

The Latino religious vote in the United States has emerged as a determining factor within the electoral landscape, standing out for its conservative inclination. As the Latino population has grown and diversified in terms of religion, its electoral behavior has gained greater relevance, influencing key elections at both the federal and state levels. Religious Latino voters tend to be, for the most part, conservative, which has had a significant impact on the political dynamics of the country. Protestant, evangelical, and Catholic religious groups among Latinos have shown a marked tendency toward the defense of traditional values, linking them to conservative political platforms, such as those of the Republican Party.

According to a survey conducted in 2020, Latino evangelicals are the group most inclined toward political conservatism. Approximately 62% of Latino evangelicals supported then-President DONALD TRUMP in the 2020 presidential elections, a figure considerably higher than the overall Latino vote, which was 38 % for Trump. This trend is largely explained by the strong defense that the Republican Party makes of principles such as religious freedom, opposition to abortion, and protection of the traditional family, central values for many Latino evangelicals.

The Latino Protestant population, mostly evangelical, has grown significantly in recent years, and with it, their political influence. According to a 2023 Pew Research Center report, there are currently around 15 million Latinos who identify as Protestant or evangelical in the United States. This group has been a key bastion in strengthening social and moral conservatism in public policies, consolidating over decades as a solid base of the Republican Party. The loyalty of this group to the Republican platforms on religious values has been a decisive factor in electoral contests, especially on issues like religious freedom and opposition to the socialist agenda in social matters.

On the other hand, Latino Catholics, although historically more aligned with the Democratic Party, have also shown a growing inclination toward conservative voting on specific issues like abortion and same-sex marriage. However, their political loyalty is more divided. According to Pew, while 68 % of Latino Catholics supported Democratic candidate JOE BIDEN in the 2020 elections, there is a significant segment, particularly among more practicing middle-class Catholics, who feel attracted to the Republican platform on matters of religious and moral values.

The role of the religious vote among Latinos is not only tied to cultural or moral issues but also to the perception that political parties reflect or ignore their deeply rooted values. In this sense, religious identity becomes a factor that influences both political affiliation and voting decisions within this group. For example, the Republican stance on freedom of worship and the defense of religious rights has strongly resonated among Latino evangelicals, who consider these issues vital to the preservation of their community identity.

Another interesting aspect to consider is the geography of the Latino religious vote. Key states with a high concentration of Latinos, such as Florida and Texas, have seen how the Latino religious vote has contributed to Republican advances in these states. In particular, the Cuban-American community in Florida, which has a significant portion of religious voters, has been decisive in consolidating the state as a Republican stronghold. In Texas, Latino evangelical voters have also played a crucial role in recent electoral contests, helping to keep the state within the Republican column.

In summary, the Latino religious vote in the United States reflects a strong conservative tendency, especially among evangelicals and, to a lesser extent, among Catholics. For the 2024 general elections, there are no definitive figures for religious voters, but the estimated participation of Latino voters in general would exceed 35 million people, of which a significant portion would correspond to the religious voter, increasingly identified with conservatism.

Coming out of the shadows

The RONALD REAGAN era

RONALD REAGAN'S presidency is remembered as a vibrant and transformative chapter in U.S. history, a period when the country once again felt strong and optimistic after the tumultuous 1970s. REAGAN, with his charisma and clear message, won the hearts of most Americans, not only for his policies but for the spirit of renewal he brought with him. When REAGAN took office in 1981, the U.S. economy was in crisis. Inflation, unemployment, and stagnation were a heavy burden for the country and for everyone. To combat this, REAGAN bet on his ambitious economic strategy, which would later be known as Reaganomics. His plan consisted of lowering taxes, trusting that citizens would use their money to invest and create jobs, and reducing government spending on social programs. It was a risky bet, and although it wasn't without criticism, it worked to revitalize the economy in the short term. The economic prosperity of the 1980s was forever associated with his administration.

One of the most iconic moments of REAGAN'S presidency was his tough stance against the Soviet Union, which he called the "Evil Empire." During his first years in the White House, REAGAN showed no intention of appeasing the Cold War. He invested colossal sums in weaponry, launching his ambitious Strategic Defense Initiative (popularly known as "Star Wars"), hoping to deter any nuclear aggression. But what was surprising was the shift that came in the second half of his presidency. When MIKHAIL GORBACHEV came to power in the Soviet Union, REAGAN saw an opportunity and, setting aside hostile rhetoric, established a dialogue that resulted in historic treaties for nuclear arms reduction. Although the collapse of the Soviet Union occurred after his term, his policy accelerated the process, and many remember him as the president who helped bring the Cold War to an end.

REAGAN also left a lasting mark on the country's immigration policy. In 1986, he signed the Immigration Reform and Control Act (IRCA), which granted amnesty to approximately 2.7 million undocumented immigrants, most of them of Latino origin, offering them a path to legalization. This was a giant step for many who had lived in the shadows and now had access to rights and protections. This law was a milestone and transformed the lives of millions of people.

The rise of the latino vote

REAGAN'S relationship with the Latino community was complex but significant. While Cuban Americans in Florida fervently supported REAGAN for his anti-communist stance (the REAGAN Doctrine), other Latino groups, such as Mexican Americans, viewed some of his economic policies, which reduced social programs, less favorably. Even so, the growth of the Latino vote began to be noticed during his years in power. His pragmatic approach to immigration reform allowed hundreds of thousands of Latinos to enter the electoral process in the following decades. Although REAGAN did not win the majority of the Latino vote, he did establish a base among conservative Latinos that has remained to this day.

Looking back, RONALD REAGAN'S presidency marked an era of change in the United States. His contagious optimism, his ability to communicate messages of hope, and his skill in facing both internal and external challenges made him a central figure in contemporary history. Reaganomics helped pull the United States out of an economic crisis; his foreign policy contributed to the end of communism; and his immigration reform changed the lives of millions of Latinos. REAGAN left behind a safer, more prosperous nation, and for many, with renewed confidence in its own future. For Latinos, REAGAN signifies the exit from the shadows and the beginning of the path to power and political influence.

Behavior of the latino vote: From REAGAN to BIDEN

Starting in 1980, Latinos began to play a prominent role in U.S. presidential elections due to demographic growth and the expansion of the electorate. This relevance has steadily grown in subsequent electoral cycles.

1980 Election (Ronald Reagan vs. Jimmy Carter)

- **Latino voters:** Around 2 million Latinos voted in this election, representing a small percentage of the total electorate, but they were already starting to gain relevance.

- **Latino support:** Jimmy Carter received the majority of the Latino vote, especially among Mexican Americans and Puerto Ricans. However, Reagan captured a significant portion of the Cuban American vote due to his firm stance against communism, solidifying his base in Florida.

- **Impact:** The Latino vote was not decisive in this election, but it marked the beginning of recognizing this group as an emerging bloc.

1984 Election (Ronald Reagan vs. Walter Mondale)

- **Latino voters:** Approximately 3 million Latinos voted in 1984, a significant increase compared to 1980.

- **Latino support:** Reagan won about 34 % of the Latino vote, consolidating the Cuban American vote and capturing part of the middle-class Latino vote, especially in states like Florida and California. Mondale won the majority of the Latino vote, but Reagan's general popularity, along with his economic and anti-communist policy, allowed him to gain more Latino support than previous Republicans.

- **Impact:** Although most Latinos voted for Mondale, Reagan's growing support among Cuban Americans was an early indication of the impact this community would have on future election.

1992 Election (Bill Clinton vs. George H.W. Bush vs. Ross Perot)

- **Latino voters:** Around 4 million Latinos participated in this election.
- **Latino support:** Bill Clinton received approximately 61 % of the Latino vote, capturing the support of Mexican Americans, Puerto Ricans, and Dominicans. The Latino vote in California was decisive for Clinton's victory, helping to shift the state consistently towards the Democrats since then.

- **Impact:** CLINTON recognized the importance of the Latino vote and adopted positions in support of civil rights and access to education, strengthening the Democratic Party's relationship with this community.

2000 Election (GEORGE W. BUSH vs. AL GORE)

- **Latino voters:** Approximately 5.9 million Latinos voted in 2000.
- **Latino support:** GEORGE W. BUSH, as former governor of Texas, received about 35 % of the national Latino vote, a considerably high figure for a Republican. His connection with Latino voters, especially in Texas and other border states, was key. However, AL GORE won the majority of the Latino vote with 62 %.
- **Impact:** Although BUSH won the presidency, the state of Florida, with its significant Cuban American community, was crucial. The votes of Latinos, especially Cuban Americans, were decisive in the tight contest for the state, where BUSH won by only 537 votes.

2008 Election (BARACK OBAMA vs. JOHN McCAIN)

- **Latino voters:** About 9.7 million Latinos participated in 2008.
- **Latino support:** OBAMA won approximately 67 % of the Latino vote, a key figure for his victory in Nevada, Colorado, New Mexico, and Florida. His focus on immigration reform and healthcare was well received by the Latino community.
- **Impact:** Latinos played a crucial role in securing key states for OBAMA, helping to turn Nevada and Colorado into Democratic states. This was a turning point for Latino support for Democrats.

2016 Election (DONALD TRUMP vs. HILLARY CLINTON)

- **Latino voters:** About 12.7 million Latinos voted in 2016.
- **Latino support:** HILLARY CLINTON won 66 % of the Latino vote, while DONALD TRUMP received around 28%. Despite TRUMP's anti-immigrant rhetoric, he managed to capture a significant portion of the Latino vote, especially among Cuban Americans in Florida and working-class Latinos in Texas.

- **Impact:** Although the Latino vote favored CLINTON, it wasn't enough to secure her victory in key states like Florida. Latinos played an important role in keeping Nevada and Colorado in the Democratic column.

2020 Election (JOE BIDEN vs. DONALD TRUMP)

- **Latino voters:** Approximately 16.6 million Latinos voted in 2020, the highest participation in U.S. history.
- **Latino support:** JOE BIDEN received 65 % of the Latino vote, while DONALD TRUMP increased his share to 38 %. BIDEN won a large portion of the Latino vote in Arizona, Nevada, and Pennsylvania, while TRUMP maintained his support in Florida, winning the majority of the Cuban American, Venezuelan, and Nicaraguan vote in the state.
- **Impact:** The Latino vote was decisive in key states like Arizona, where it helped BIDEN win the state by a narrow margin. In Nevada and Colorado, Latinos also played an important role in the Democratic victory. On the other hand, in Florida, the increase in Latino support for TRUMP was key to keeping the state in the Republican column.

Over the decades, the Latino vote has evolved from being a small and marginal voice to becoming one of the most influential blocs in U.S. presidential elections. In the 1980s, Latinos were an emerging group, little considered by political strategists. However, over time, their presence has grown notably, and by 2020, 16.6 million Latinos participated in the elections, marking a milestone in the country's political history.

This growth not only reflects the numerical increase but the consolidation of a political identity that is increasingly diverse and active at the heart of American democracy.

The latino vote decides

In recent years, the Latino vote has gone from being an emerging bloc to becoming a crucial factor in the outcome of many elections, especially in those where victory margins are narrow. Although historically underestimated, its consolidation as an influential electoral group has been evidenced in several presidential and state cycles, where their participation has been decisive in the final result.

The impact of the Latino vote has become particularly visible in "battleground" states such as Florida, Nevada, Arizona, and Texas, where the high concentration of Latino voters has tipped the balance in close contests. In states like Florida, the Cuban American community has proven to be key for Republicans, while Mexican Americans in the Southwest tend to support Democrats more.

Tight elections in the last two decades have shown that, although the Latino vote doesn't always mobilize uniformly, its importance continues to grow. Factors such as origin diversity, key issues affecting them, and participation rates define how this group can change the outcome of an election. Analyzing these cases allows us to understand how the influence of the Latino vote has not only grown but has consolidated as a fundamental pillar in the electoral game of the United States.

2000 Presidential election: Florida and cuban americans

Case: Florida (George W. Bush vs. Al Gore)

The 2000 presidential election was one of the closest in U.S. history. The contest's outcome came down to a single state: Florida, where victory margins were extremely narrow.

- **Latino vote in Florida:** In Florida, Cuban Americans, who form a solid and conservative electoral bloc, played a decisive role. Approximately 80 % of the Cuban American vote favored George W. Bush, helping tip the state in his favor. Bush won Florida by only 537 votes after the recount, highlighting the importance of this electoral group in a close election.

- **Decisiveness of the latino vote:** Without the significant support of Cuban Americans in South Florida, it is likely that Al Gore would have won the state and, therefore, the presidency. This case demonstrates how a Latino subgroup can be decisive in a competitive state.

2008 Presidential Election: Nevada and New Mexico

Case: Nevada and New Mexico (Barack Obama vs. John McCain)

In the 2008 election, the Latino vote was decisive in several Southwestern states, where the Latino community, mostly of Mexican origin, represented a significant percentage of the electorate.

- **Nevada:** In this state, Latinos made up about 15 % of the electorate and overwhelmingly supported Obama, with 76 % of the Latino vote. This support was crucial for Obama's victory in Nevada, a state where victory margins are usually tight.
- **New Mexico:** Here, Latinos represented nearly 40 % of the electorate and also supported Obama by a large margin, with about 69 % of the Latino vote. The victory in New Mexico was significant in securing Obama's triumph in the Southwest.
- **Decisiveness of the latino vote:** In both states, Latino support was key to Obama's margin of victory, showing that in states where Latinos make up a significant part of the electorate, their vote can tip close elections.

2012 Presidential Election: Colorado and Nevada

Case: Colorado and Nevada (Barack Obama vs. Mitt Romney)

In 2012, Barack Obama's re-election was reinforced by the Latino vote, especially in "battleground" states like Colorado and Nevada, where victory margins were relatively tight.

- **Colorado:** Latinos made up about 14 % of the electorate in Colorado, and Obama won 75 % of the Latino vote in the state. Latino participation was decisive, as Obama won the state by only 5 percentage points, a relatively narrow margin in a presidential election.
- **Nevada:** In Nevada, where Latinos made up about 19 % of the electorate, Obama won 71% of the Latino vote, which was decisive in securing his victory in the state.
- **Decisiveness of the latino vote:** The Latino vote was decisive in these two key states, which were battlegrounds in the contest. Without the overwhelming support of Latino voters, it is likely that the results would have been much closer or that Romney would have had a greater chance of winning.

2016 Presidential Election: Florida and Texas

Case: Florida and Texas (Donald Trump vs. Hillary Clinton)

Donald Trump's election in 2016 was a surprise to some, and his victory was partly due to his ability to capture part of the Latino vote in key states.

- **Florida:** Although Hillary Clinton won the majority of the Latino vote in Florida, Donald Trump received about 35 % of the Latino vote, including important portions of the Cuban American and Venezuelan vote in South Florida. This support was crucial for Trump's victory in Florida, where he won by a relatively small margin of 1.2 percentage points.

- **Texas:** In Texas, Trump improved the Republican performance among Latinos in border areas, where he captured a considerable portion of the Latino vote, particularly among Texas Mexicans. Although Texas was not as competitive as other states, Latino support was key to keeping the state in Republican hands.

- **Decisiveness of the latino vote:** In Florida, the Latino vote was crucial in securing Trump's victory. Without Cuban American support, it is likely that the results would have been different. In Texas, the growing Latino participation continues to be a key factor in determining whether the state will remain Republican or become competitive in the future.

2020 Presidential Election: Arizona and Nevada

Case: Arizona and Nevada (Joe Biden vs. Donald Trump)

In 2020, the Latino vote was key to Joe Biden's victory in Southwestern "battleground" states, particularly in Arizona and Nevada.

- **Arizona:** Latinos made up about 23 % of the electorate in Arizona, and Biden won 63 % of the Latino vote in the state. This support was crucial, as Biden won Arizona by a very narrow margin of about 10,500 votes, or 0.3 percentage points.

- **Nevada:** In Nevada, Latinos made up 19 % of the electorate, and Biden won 67 % of the Latino vote, which was key to his victory in this state. Nevada was one of the most competitive states, and the Latino vote was fundamental to the final result.

- **Decisiveness of the latino vote:** Without strong Latino support in Arizona and Nevada, it is likely that Biden would not have won these states. The Latino vote was decisive in both contests, as the victory margins were small enough that Latino participation and electoral behavior tipped the balance.

The latino vote grows and multiplies

The Latino vote has steadily increased in recent decades. In 2020, 16.6 million Latinos participated in the elections, representing 13.3 % of the total electorate. This number is expected to continue growing as more Latinos reach voting age. By 2030, it is projected that Latinos will make up nearly 18 % of the national electorate, making them a decisive group in future elections.

This growth is driven by several factors, including:

- The high birth rate among Latinos compared to other groups.
- Immigration, although only U.S. citizens can vote, meaning there is a delay in voting eligibility for immigrants.
- The expansion of the second and third generation of Latinos born in the United States.

Voting patterns and diversity

Although Latinos tend to lean more towards the Democratic Party, the Latino vote is not monolithic. The diversity within the Latino community, which includes Mexicans, Cubans, Puerto Ricans, Venezuelans, Central Americans, and South Americans, generates different priorities and voting behaviors.

For example:

- **Mexicans:** They tend to vote mostly for Democrats, particularly in states like California, Arizona, Nevada, and Texas.
- **Cuban Americans:** Traditionally, they have supported the Republican Party, especially in Florida, due to their historical opposition to FIDEL CASTRO's regime and their support for a hardline foreign policy towards Cuba.

- **Puerto Ricans:** They tend to vote for Democrats, especially in states like Florida and New York, where healthcare and immigration policies are key issues.
- **Venezuelans:** In Florida, a considerable part of the Venezuelan diaspora has shown support for the Republican Party due to the hardline stance against the socialist regime of Nicolás Maduro.

States where the latino vote carries more weight

Florida

- **Latino population:** Approximately 5.6 million Latinos.
- **Importance of the latino vote:** Florida is one of the most competitive states in presidential elections, and its Latino vote is extremely important due to the diversity of the Latino community in the state. South Florida is home to large populations of Cubans, Venezuelans, and Nicaraguans, who have historically supported the Republican Party due to its foreign policy toward their countries of origin. In the 2020 elections, Donald Trump managed to capture a significant portion of the Latino vote in Florida.
- **Why it's important:** Florida is a state with 29 electoral votes. The high concentration of Latinos in the southern part of the state makes it a key place where candidates from both parties focus on winning the Latino vote. Elections in Florida tend to be decided by narrow margins, making each segment of the electorate, especially Latinos, crucial.

Texas

- **Latino population:** More than 11.4 million, representing more than 40 % of the state's total population.
- **Importance of the latino vote:** Although Texas has historically been a Republican state, the growth of the Latino population has made the state increasingly competitive. In the 2020 elections, Joe Biden received a high percentage of the Latino vote in Texas, but Donald Trump also made significant advances in border areas, capturing a larger portion of the Latino vote than in previous elections.
- **Why it's important:** Texas has 38 electoral votes, and the growth of the Latino population is transforming the state's political landscape.

Arizona

- **Latino population:** Approximately 2.4 million, representing about 30 % of the population.
- **Importance of the latino vote:** Arizona is a state that has experienced political change in recent years, shifting from a Republican stronghold to a competitive state. In the 2020 elections, the Latino vote was key to JOE BIDEN's victory, as he won the state by a very narrow margin.
- **Why it's important:** Arizona has 11 electoral votes, and its growing Latino population has played a decisive role in the state's political transformation. Arizona's Latino community is mostly of Mexican origin.

Nevada

- **Latino population:** Approximately 900,000 voters, representing 29 % of the state's population.
- **Importance of the latino vote:** In 2020, the Latino vote was crucial to JOE BIDEN's victory in Nevada, where he won with 67 % of the Latino vote. The Latino community is mainly of Mexican and Central American origin.
- **Why it's important:** Nevada has 6 electoral votes, and although it is a small state, its Latino electorate has been decisive in close elections. Campaigns focus on issues like healthcare, education, and the economy, which are priorities for Latino voters.

Colorado

- **Latino population:** Approximately 1.3 million, representing about 22 % of the state's population.
- **Importance of the latino vote:** Colorado is an increasingly competitive state. In the 2020 elections, JOE BIDEN won with about 70 % of the Latino vote.
- **Why it's important** Although Colorado only has 9 electoral votes, its growing Latino population has been key in presidential elections. Immigration and labor rights are important issues for Latino voters in Colorado.

Georgia

- **Latino population:** About 1 million, representing approximately 10 % of the population.
- **Importance of the latino vote:** In 2020, Georgia was one of the most surprising states where the Latino vote, along with the African American vote, was key to JOE BIDEN's victory. The rapid growth of the Latino community has made Georgia an increasingly competitive state, and it is expected that the Latino vote will continue to play an important role in future elections.
- **Why it's important:** Georgia has 16 electoral votes. As the Latino population continues to grow, this group is expected to remain a decisive factor in this state, which has shifted from a Republican stronghold to a "battleground" state.

Latinos surpassed African Americans as the largest minority in the United States around the year 2000. With more than 62 million Latinos in the country in 2020, this community represents approximately 19 % of the total population.

The fact that Latinos are the largest minority in the United States means that their vote is crucial in determining the outcome of presidential elections, as any party that manages to attract and mobilize this group can secure victory in key states. Additionally, the impact of the Latino vote will continue to grow as more Latinos register to vote and become politically involved.

Political campaigns: Adjustments to win the latino vote

In recent decades, both the Republican and Democratic parties have recognized the growing importance of the Latino vote and have adjusted their strategies to capture this key segment of the electorate. There are 34 million eligible voters (2020), and logically, winning them over has become a strategic priority for both parties' campaigns.

How do they do it?
The democratic party and the latino vote

Historically, the Democratic Party has received the majority of the Latino vote, capturing between 60 % and 70 % of this bloc in presidential elections since the 1990s. Democrats have focused their efforts on key issues for many Latinos, such as immigration reform and healthcare.

- **Immigration and DACA**: They have championed proposals that include a path to citizenship for undocumented immigrants and protection for Dreamers under the DACA program. This has been especially attractive to Latino voters, many of whom have family members affected by immigration policies.

- **Economy and education**: Democrats have emphasized their proposals to improve public education and expand economic opportunities for Latinos, advocating for better wages, job opportunities, and access to healthcare.

Mobilization strategies

EIn recent election cycles, Democrats have intensified their focus on Latino voter registration and mobilization. Sympathetic organizations such as Mi Familia Vota, Voto Latino, and UnidosUS have worked closely with Democrats to increase Latino participation, particularly among young and first-generation voters.

Digital platforms and social media

The Democratic Party has adopted an intensive social media strategy to reach Latino voters, as Latinos in general have a high adoption rate of platforms like Facebook, Instagram, Twitter, and YouTube. The use of bilingual content and campaigns specifically targeting subgroups within the Latino community, such as Mexicans, Puerto Ricans, and Venezuelans, has been key in the Democratic digital strategy.

In the 2020 elections, Democrats invested significantly in digital advertising, particularly in battleground states like Arizona, Florida, and Nevada. In total, the Democratic National Committee (DNC) spent more than $80 million on efforts targeting Latino voters.

Traditional media: Radio and television

Democrats have also used traditional media such as television and radio, especially on Spanish-language channels like Univision, Telemundo, and local radio stations. These platforms remain influential in the Latino

community, particularly among older Latinos and those who prefer consuming media in Spanish.

In 2020, JOE BIDEN's campaign invested about $21 million in television ads targeting Latinos, a figure that represented a significant increase compared to previous cycles.

The Republican party and the latino vote

Traditionally, the Republican Party has had some difficulty capturing the majority of the Latino vote, mainly due to its more legalistic stance on issues like immigration. However, until the 2020 elections, Republicans had significantly improved their performance among certain Latino subgroups, such as Cuban Americans, Venezuelans, and Nicaraguans, who respond positively to the Republican Party's ideology of economic freedom, conservative values, and a tough foreign policy towards leftist regimes in Latin America.

- **Foreign policy and communism:** Republicans have been particularly successful in attracting Latinos who have a firm stance against socialism and communism, especially in Florida. The Cuban American community, as well as the growing Venezuelan and Nicaraguan communities, have shown strong support for Republican candidates due to the party's firm stance against the regimes in Cuba and Venezuela. DONALD TRUMP capitalized on this narrative in 2020, allowing him to increase his percentage of the Latino vote in Florida.

- **Economy and small businesses:** Republicans have emphasized pro-business policies, promoting tax cuts and deregulation, issues that resonate with many Latino small business owners. TRUMP's campaign also invested resources in highlighting the economic benefits that Republican policies offer the Latino community.

Mobilization strategies

Republicans have worked to expand their base among Latinos, particularly those with conservative and religious leanings. Groups like Latinos for TRUMP have played a crucial role in attracting conservative Latino voters, registering millions of Latinos in the Republican Party.

Chapter 5

In 2020, Donald Trump's campaign significantly increased its focus on Latinos, with a strategy centered on traditional values, pre-pandemic economic growth, and opposition to socialism, which strongly resonated with Cuban American and Venezuelan voters in Florida.

Digital platforms and social media

Republicans have also effectively used social media to reach Latino voters. During the 2020 elections, Trump's campaign invested aggressively in Facebook and YouTube, launching ads in Spanish and using Latino influencers to convey their messages. Trump invested more than $20 million in digital advertising targeting Latinos in key states.

- One effective Republican strategy was the use of social media to inform about the Marxist inclination of Democratic candidates, particularly in Florida, where ads linking them to socialist regimes had a strong impact on the Cuban and Venezuelan communities.
- Spanish-language podcasts have also played an important role in informing this audience.
- Community events and town halls are very popular among Republicans, where candidates can speak directly to Latino voters and discuss community issues.

Traditional media: Radio and television

The Republican Party has also invested in traditional media, especially in Spanish-language radio, which remains influential among older and conservative Latinos who prefer consuming media in Spanish. In states like Florida and Texas, local stations that broadcast in Spanish play a crucial role in shaping public opinion.

In Florida, Trump's 2020 campaign made a strong investment in local stations that appealed to Cuban Americans and other conservative Latinos.

Republicans invested more than $9 million in Spanish-language media ads in Florida in 2020, highlighting their efforts to attract key Latino voters in this crucial state.

Investment in the latino vote vs. the anglo vote

States with the most investment

The states where the most money is spent to attract the Latino vote are those considered battlegrounds in presidential elections:

- **Florida:** It remains one of the states with the most investment due to the diversity of the Latino vote (Cuban Americans, Puerto Ricans, Venezuelans). TRUMP'S 2020 campaign invested about $9 million in Spanish-language media alone, and this figure will likely increase in 2024.
- **Arizona:** With a Latino population representing 30 % of the electorate, significant investment is expected in 2024, similar to what happened in 2020, where the Latino vote was decisive in BIDEN'S victory.
- **Nevada:** Another key state where Latinos make up almost 30 % of the electorate. Campaigns typically allocate millions of dollars in Spanish-language ads and mobilization efforts to capture the Latino vote.
- **Texas:** Although it has traditionally been a Republican state, its growing Latino population is generating greater investment in advertising targeting Latino voters, with a view to mobilizing them in urban and border areas.

Comparison of investments

Despite the growing focus on Latino voters, investment in the Latino community remains significantly lower compared to investment in Anglo voters.

- In the 2020 elections, it is estimated that both campaigns (Democratic and Republican) spent a total of more than $750 million on advertising targeting Anglo voters, while the total investment in the Latino vote was around $100 million. This shows a significant disparity, despite the fact that Latinos make up an increasingly larger proportion of the electorate.
- Compared to Anglo voters, parties have allocated only 13 % of their advertising spending to Latino voters, a very low figure considering that Latinos represent about 13.3 % of the electorate.

The difference in investment can be explained by several factors:

- **Historical:** Latinos have traditionally had lower voter turnout rates compared to other groups, leading parties to allocate fewer resources to this electoral bloc.

- **Segmentation and reach:** Anglo voters tend to be a more homogeneous group in terms of media preferences and platforms, making it easier to reach them with mass campaigns. In contrast, Latinos are a diverse group with generational, cultural, and linguistic differences that require more specific and segmented marketing strategies, which can limit the scale of investment.

Examples of specific campaigns targeting latino voters and their impact on the results

In the 2020 presidential elections, both the Democratic and Republican parties implemented specific campaigns to attract Latino voters, recognizing their growing importance as a decisive electoral bloc in key states. Below are some examples of specific campaigns targeting the Latino community, along with their impact on electoral results.

Barack Obama's 2012 Campaign: "Latinos for Obama"

Description

During Barack Obama's 2012 re-election campaign, his team launched the "Latinos for Obama" campaign, which focused on priority issues for the Latino community, such as immigration reform, healthcare, and access to education. The campaign was a combination of traditional and digital advertising, as well as grassroots mobilization efforts in states with large Latino populations like Nevada, Colorado, and Florida.

- **Spanish-language advertising:** Obama's team launched a series of ads in Spanish highlighting his commitment to DACA (Deferred Action for Childhood Arrivals) and his efforts to advance immigration reform.

- **Use of social media:** Obama used platforms like Facebook and YouTube to reach younger Latino voters, with culturally relevant content and in Spanish.

Impact

The campaign was a great success, with OBAMA capturing 71 % of the Latino vote in 2012. In states like Nevada, where Latinos made up 19 % of the electorate, their support was crucial in securing victory. In Colorado, the Latino vote was also key, as OBAMA won 75 % of the Latino vote, significantly contributing to his margin of victory in the state.

Final outcome: OBAMA won comfortably in key states where the Latino vote was decisive, consolidating his victory nationally and demonstrating the effectiveness of a campaign specifically targeting this electoral group.

Donald Trump's 2020 Campaign: "Latinos for TRUMP"

Description

In the 2020 elections, DONALD TRUMP's campaign launched an intensive strategy targeting conservative Latinos under the slogan "Latinos for TRUMP." The campaign focused on several key issues:

- **Opposition to socialism:** In states like Florida, TRUMP's campaign directed specific ads at Cuban Americans and Venezuelans, linking the Democratic Party to socialism and highlighting the negative effects of the regimes in Cuba and Venezuela.
- **Economic freedom:** TRUMP also highlighted his handling of the economy before the pandemic, focusing on traditional values, economic freedom, and job creation, messages that resonated with many conservative Latinos.
- **Digital platforms and social media:** TRUMP's campaign was very active on Facebook and YouTube, where it invested millions of dollars in Spanish-language ads, many of which focused on warning about the dangers of socialism.

Impact

The "Latinos for TRUMP" campaign was particularly successful in Florida, where TRUMP won around 47 % of the Latino vote, a significant increase compared to the 2016 elections. His performance among Cuban Americans and Venezuelans in South Florida was crucial for his victory in the state.

Final outcome: Nationally, TRUMP improved his performance among Latinos, capturing 32 % of the Latino vote. In Texas, TRUMP also improved his performance in traditionally Democratic border areas, obtaining a significant portion of the Latino vote in the Rio Grande Valley.

JOE BIDEN'S 2020 Campaign: "Todos con BIDEN"

Description

JOE BIDEN'S 2020 campaign launched the "Todos con BIDEN" initiative, specifically targeting Latino voters. This campaign focused on issues such as immigration reform, economic recovery after the pandemic, and social justice. BIDEN also tried to connect with younger generations of Latinos through digital platforms.

- **Spanish-language ads:** The campaign launched a series of Spanish-language ads on Hispanic networks and other Spanish-speaking platforms. In these ads, BIDEN pledged to restore DACA and fight for immigration reform.
- **Digital platforms:** The campaign heavily invested in social media platforms like Instagram, Facebook, and YouTube to reach younger Latino voters. The ads focused on health issues and the pandemic response, important aspects for the Latino community, which was greatly affected by the COVID-19 pandemic.

Impact

The campaign was successful in several key states. BIDEN won 65 % of the Latino vote nationally, with particularly strong results in states like Arizona and Nevada:

- **Arizona:** BIDEN won 63 % of the Latino vote, which was crucial to his victory in the state, as he won by only 10,500 votes. The mobilization of young Latinos in Arizona was key, and the focus on social media and the commitment to immigration reform resonated with this group.
- **Nevada:** In Nevada, BIDEN received 67 % of the Latino vote, which was fundamental for his victory in this state.

Final outcome: The success of the "Todos con BIDEN" campaign helped secure his victory in battleground states with a large Latino population.

Hillary Clinton's 2016 Campaign: "I'm With Her"

Description

In 2016, Hillary Clinton launched a campaign targeting Latinos under the slogan "I'm With Her." The campaign focused on issues like immigration reform, DACA, and equal opportunities. Clinton invested in Spanish-language ads and events targeting Latino voters in states like Nevada, Florida, and Texas.

- **Spanish-Language TV and radio ads:** Clinton launched television ads in Spanish on Hispanic networks, highlighting her support for Dreamers and her commitment to the Latino community.
- **Grassroots mobilization:** Clinton's campaign worked with Democratic-affiliated organizations like "Voto Latino" to register new voters and mobilize young Latinos.

Impact

Despite receiving 66 % of the Latino vote nationally, Clinton's campaign failed to mobilize enough Latino voters in key states like Florida, where Donald Trump won a significant portion of the Cuban American vote.

Final outcome: Although Clinton won a majority of the Latino vote, it wasn't enough to counter Trump's strong support among conservative Latinos in Florida and Texas, contributing to her defeat in these states.

I'm switching parties! Latinos and party affinity

"Faithful forever" does not seem to be the best description of Latino voters regarding loyalty to their party affiliation. Nor is it solid or predictable like that of other electoral groups. And although historically most Latinos have tended to support the Democratic Party, it cannot be said that they are entirely loyal to one party. The electoral behavior of Latinos has shown considerable flexibility, depending on factors such as the economy, immigration policy, and cultural or social issues.

Traditionally, Latinos have voted in greater proportion for Democratic candidates due to the perception that this party promotes policies that favor minorities.

However, in recent years, significant sectors of the Latino community have shown a tendency to switch parties, especially toward the Republican

Party. This shift has been particularly observed in more conservative or working-class Latino communities in Texas and Florida.

Factors influencing party switching

- **Economy:** Many working-class Latinos, especially small business owners, are attracted to the Republican proposal of lower taxes and deregulation, which favors job creation and economic growth.
- **Foreign policy:** Latinos who have fled communist regimes in Latin America, such as Cuban Americans and Venezuelans, find an ally in the Republican Party in their fight against communism and socialism.
- **Social issues:** Conservative Latinos, especially those with strong religious convictions, have been drawn to the Republican message on issues such as abortion and traditional family values.
- **Security and border control:** In border areas of Texas and Arizona, some Latinos support stricter Republican policies in terms of border security. Although immigration is a priority issue for many Latinos, those living near the border often support greater control over illegal immigration, as well as the strengthening of law enforcement in their communities. This approach is seen by some as a way to maintain local security and curb crime.

How to win the latino vote

Due to its peculiarities and characteristics, it is becoming increasingly difficult to win the Latino vote in every election. Latinos now understand that their vote counts, and they stopped being the "poor relatives" of American elections long ago. Therefore, they demand, and in each election, fewer voters are swayed by organizations that manipulate them to vote for one candidate or another. That being the case, many elected officials and candidates have also made mistakes in their strategy to win the Latino vote.

To win the Latino vote, political candidates must consider several cultural, social, and economic factors that are key to authentically connecting with this community. There are certain actions that, if carried out, can alienate or lose the support of Latino voters. Below are some things a political candidate should never do if they want to capture the Latino vote:

Ignore the diversity of the latino community

Latinos are not a monolithic bloc; the community is extremely diverse in terms of origin, culture, history, and priorities. Ignoring this diversity and treating Latinos as a homogeneous group can be harmful.

- **Common mistake:** Grouping Latinos as if they all share the same interests and priorities. Mexican Americans in California may have different concerns than Cuban Americans in Florida or Puerto Ricans in New York.
- **Consequence:** The lack of focus on the particularities of different Latino subgroups can make the candidate seem disconnected or indifferent to their specific concerns.

Avoid or ignore the issue of immigration

Immigration remains one of the most important issues for many Latino voters, even for those who are not first-generation immigrants. A candidate who avoids talking about clear policies in this area or uses negative language toward immigrants can alienate this electoral bloc.

- **Common mistake:** Until 2020, using a tough stance on immigration without considering the emotional and family connection many Latinos have with immigration. (After the 2024 immigration crisis created by the BIDEN-HARRIS open border policies, which allowed approximately 10 million illegal immigrants to enter the United States, the tough stance on illegal immigration is now significantly supported by the Latino community.)
- **Consequence:** Latinos may see these positions as direct attacks on their communities, leading them to reject the candidate.

Underestimate the importance of the economy

Although immigration is an important issue, the economy remains the most important issue for Latinos. Candidates who do not address employment, economic security, and small business growth may lose Latino support.

- **Common mistake:** Assuming that Latinos only care about immigration issues and not focusing on job creation or access to economic opportunities.

- **Consequence:** Latinos seeking financial stability and economic growth may lean toward candidates who focus on strong economic policies, regardless of the party.

Ignore cultural representation

A candidate seeking the Latino vote must show a genuine understanding of the culture and values of this community. Ignoring or underestimating the value of cultural representation and respect can be harmful.

- **Common mistake:** Trying to capture the Latino vote through superficial gestures without a genuine commitment to the issues that really matter.
- **Consequence:** Latinos may perceive these actions as insincere and opportunistic, which can cause the candidate to lose credibility.

Promise without delivering

Candidates who make promises to the Latino community, such as immigration reform or improvements in access to healthcare and education, must be willing to fulfill them. Latinos have heard repeated promises over the years without seeing real changes, leading to distrust.

- **Common mistake:** Making significant promises during the campaign and then not prioritizing them once in office.
- **Consequence:** The lack of action can lead to disappointment and detachment from the Latino community, affecting voter turnout and trust in the candidate.

Not making an authentic communication effort

Latinos consume a wide variety of media, including social media, Spanish-language television, and radio. A candidate who does not use these platforms to effectively reach Latinos misses a great opportunity to communicate with this electorate.

- **Common mistake:** Not running campaigns in Spanish or not using media popular among Latinos, such as Hispanic networks or local Spanish-language radio stations.
- **Consequence:** The lack of proper communication can give the impression that the candidate is not interested in reaching the Latino community.

Political representation of latinos in elected offices

The political representation of Latinos in the U.S. has grown exponentially in recent years, from the federal Congress to state legislatures and local and county mayors. This increase is largely due to the growth of the Latino population and greater political participation, motivated by key issues for Hispanics. This increase is most evident in states with large Hispanic populations like Florida, New York, Nevada, California, Arizona, and Pennsylvania. In many cases, Latinos have won elections thanks to the Hispanic vote, particularly in states and cities with large Latino populations, demonstrating the growing power of this electoral bloc in U.S. politics.

Florida: Growth of latino representation

Florida is a key state for Latino representation, driven mainly by the Cuban American community and other Latino groups, such as Venezuelans and Nicaraguans.

- **Congress:** Florida has sent an increasing number of Latino representatives to Congress. María Elvira Salazar, Carlos Gimenez, Mario Díaz-Balart, and Senator Marco Rubio are examples of Cuban American Latino leaders elected with strong support from the Hispanic vote.
- **State Legislature:** In Florida's legislature, Latinos have gained greater representation in recent years. In 2020, Latinos held about 20 % of the seats in the state legislature, a considerable figure given the weight of the Latino population in the state.
- **Mayorships:** Francis Suárez, of Cuban origin, was elected mayor of Miami in 2017 and has been re-elected with broad support from the Cuban American community.

Did they win because of the Hispanic vote?

Yes, in Florida, the Cuban American vote has been key to the success of Latino candidates. In South Florida, particularly in Miami-Dade, Latinos have played a crucial role in Republican victories in state and national elections.

New York: Advances in latino representation

New York has seen a steady increase in Latino representation, particularly among Puerto Ricans and Dominicans.

- **Congress:** Latino leaders like Nydia Velázquez (of Puerto Rican origin) have held key seats in the House of Representatives. Adriano Espaillat, the first Dominican-origin congressman, has been a prominent figure since his election in 2016, and Nicole Malliotakis of Cuban origin.

- **State Legislature:** Latinos have also increased their presence in New York's Assembly and Senate, representing the interests of Hispanic communities in the Bronx, Manhattan, and other areas with a high density of Latino populations.

Did they win because of the Hispanic vote?

Yes, in New York, the Hispanic vote has been crucial, especially in urban districts like the Bronx and Upper Manhattan, where the Dominican and Puerto Rican populations are very influential

Nevada: Growing representation

In Nevada, Latinos have played a key role in state and federal politics, pushing Latino leaders into important positions.

- **Congress:** Catherine Cortez Masto, of Mexican origin, became the first Latina woman in the U.S. Senate after winning her seat in 2016, with strong support from the Latino vote in Nevada.

- **State Legislature:** In Nevada, Latinos have gained representation in the state legislature, currently holding about 20 % of the seats, reflecting the growing political power of Latinos in the state.

Did they win because of the Hispanic vote?

Yes, in Nevada, the Latino vote has been crucial in the victories of leaders like Cortez Masto and other Latino candidates, particularly in urban areas like Las Vegas, where Latinos make up 29 % of the population.

California: A leader in latino representation

California, the state with the largest Latino population in the country, has been a leader in electing Latinos to public office at all levels.

- **Congress:** California has sent several Latinos to Congress, such as Xavier Becerra and Raul Ruiz, who have been important leaders in the House of Representatives.

- **State Legislature:** Latinos have achieved significant representation in the state legislature, holding more than 25 % of the seats in both chambers, reflecting the state's predominantly Latino population (39 %).
- **Mayorships:** In Los Angeles, Antonio Villaraigosa was the first Latino mayor in more than a century, while ERIC GARCETTI, of Mexican descent, was elected in 2013.

Did they win because of the Hispanic vote?

Yes, in California, the Hispanic vote has been decisive in the election of many Latino leaders, particularly in districts where the Latino population is predominant, such as Los Angeles and the Central Valley.

Arizona: Growth of latino representation

In Arizona, a state with a growing Latino population, Latinos have gained greater political representation in recent decades.

- **Congress:** RUBÉN GALLEGO, a congressman of Mexican and Colombian origin, has been a key figure in Arizona politics since 2015.
- **State Legislature:** Latinos have increased their presence in Arizona's state legislature, with 19 % of the seats held by Latinos in 2021.

Did they win because of the Hispanic vote?

Yes, the Latino vote has been crucial in Arizona, particularly in districts like Tucson, where the Latino population represents a significant portion of the electorate.

Pennsylvania: Growing latino representation

Although Pennsylvania does not have as large a Latino population as other states, the growth of the Hispanic community –especially in Philadelphia and Allentown– has boosted political representation in recent years. And although there are currently no Latino congressmen or federal senators representing this state, the presence of Latino legislators in the state legislature has grown.

- **State Legislature:** Names like DANILO BURGOS (D) from the 197th district of Philadelphia, MANUEL GUZMÁN Jr. (D) from the 127th district of Berks County, and JOSÉ GIRAL (D) from the 180th district of Philadelphia reflect the growing influence of Latinos in Pennsylvania's state politics.

Did they win because of the Hispanic vote?

In Pennsylvania, the Hispanic vote has begun to play a more important role in cities with significant concentrations of Latinos, although its impact is not yet as great as in other states.

The future of the latino vote: Challenges and opportunities

The future of the Latino vote in the United States is projected to be a key force in the country's politics, marked by unprecedented demographic growth and an increase in electoral and political participation. Over the past decades, Latinos have gone from being a marginal group to becoming a crucial electoral bloc, capable of influencing the outcome of presidential, midterm, and local elections. Their participation has grown significantly, especially in states like Arizona, Nevada, Texas, and Florida, where the concentration of Latino voters has had a decisive impact on results.

In the 2020 presidential election, more than 16.6 million Latinos exercised their right to vote, a significant increase compared to previous elections. This corresponds to a participation rate of 53.7 % of eligible Latinos, still lower than other ethnic groups like African Americans and Anglo-Saxons but showing an upward trend. This growth reflects the demographic increase of the Latino population, which today represents 19 % of the country's total population, making it the largest minority in the United States. The impact of the Latino vote has been most evident in key states, where the mobilization of this group has decided tight contests, such as Joe Biden's victory in Arizona and Nevada.

Politically, Latino representation has also grown significantly. In the United States Congress, more than 40 Latino congressmen hold seats in the House of Representatives and the Senate, from states like California, Texas, Florida, Arizona, and Nevada. These legislators not only represent the Latino community but also lead debates on issues affecting the entire country, such as the economy, immigration laws, and access to healthcare. This increase in political representation is also reflected at the state and local levels, where more Latinos are being elected as state legislators, mayors, and councilors. States like California and Texas have seen an increase in the presence of Latino leaders in their state legislatures, while in cities with a strong Latino presence, like Los Angeles and Miami, Latinos hold key public office positions.

Despite these advances, the Latino vote faces several challenges. One of the most important is the voter turnout rate, which, although growing, remains lower than that of other ethnic groups. Language barriers and lack of access to electoral information are some of the factors that hinder full Latino participation.

The future of the Latino vote is full of opportunities. As more Latinos register to vote and participate in elections, their influence on U.S. politics will continue to grow. Both parties, Democrats and Republicans, are adjusting their strategies to capture this crucial vote, recognizing that Latinos are not a monolithic group and that their interests are diverse and constantly evolving. Latino representation in Congress, as well as in state and local governments, is expected to continue increasing, allowing the Latino community to have a stronger voice in political decisions that affect the entire country.

Chapter 6

Florida:
model of
latino vote
power

The history of the Latino vote in Florida has been crucial in understanding the state's political evolution from the time of RONALD REAGAN to the present with JOE BIDEN. For decades, Florida has been one of the most contested states in presidential elections, and the Latino vote has played an increasingly important role in defining its political color, evolving from a more diverse state in its leanings to becoming solidly red in recent elections.

During RONALD REAGAN's presidency in the 1980s, Florida already had a considerable Cuban-American population, particularly in the Miami-Dade County area. The Cuban-Americans, who had arrived in several waves after the Cuban Revolution of 1959, aligned firmly with the Republicans due to REAGAN's anti-communist stance. This group overwhelmingly voted for Reagan, drawn by his strong rhetoric against FIDEL CASTRO's regime and his staunch defense of freedom and capitalism. Throughout the 1980s and 1990s, Cuban-Americans remained loyal to the Republican Party, influencing key elections in the state.

As the Latino population in Florida grew, it also diversified. In the 1990s and 2000s, large waves of Puerto Ricans began to settle primarily in the Orlando area and central Florida. Unlike Cuban-Americans, Puerto Ricans have tended to vote more for Democrats due to their support for social welfare, education, and public health policies. Despite this inclination towards Democrats, the Puerto Rican vote has not always been as consistent or decisive as the Cuban-American vote.

The 2000 presidential election marked a crucial moment in Florida's electoral history. The state's vote recount, which determined GEORGE W. BUSH's victory over AL GORE, made it clear that Florida would be a state where every vote counted. In that election, Latinos, especially Cuban-Americans, largely voted for BUSH, helping to secure his narrow victory. As elections progressed in the following decades, the Latino vote consolidated as a decisive factor not only in Florida but also in presidential elections nationally.

In the 2016 elections, Donald Trump managed to capture a significant portion of the Cuban-American vote, thanks to his hardline stance against communism and the Raúl Castro regime. Although Latinos generally favored Hillary Clinton, Trump solidified his support in the Cuban-American community and among more conservative Latino sectors, such as many Nicaraguans and Venezuelans who opposed the regimes in their countries of origin. In the 2020 elections, Trump increased his support among Latinos in Florida, winning about 52 % of the Latino vote in the state, while Joe Biden won 47 %. This support was bolstered by strong Cuban-American backing and other groups like Venezuelans and Nicaraguans, who resonated with the Republican discourse on freedom and the fight against socialism.

Regarding the Latino population, Florida has more than 2.6 million registered Latino voters. The Cuban-American community remains the most influential, representing 29 % of Latinos in Florida, concentrated in the southern part of the state, especially in Miami-Dade County. Meanwhile, Puerto Ricans, who make up 28% of Latino voters, are primarily found in central Florida, particularly in areas like Orlando and Kissimmee. Other growing groups include Venezuelans, who have seen a sharp increase over the past two decades due to the political crisis in Venezuela, as well as Colombians and Nicaraguans, who also concentrate in South Florida.

Florida's political evolution toward a red state in recent elections is largely due to the consolidation of the Cuban-American vote and the growing support from other conservative Latino groups, who have favored Republican candidates.

Cuban immigration

Cuban immigration to the United States since 1960 has been one of the most influential within the Latino community, both in terms of numbers and political and social impact. From the triumph of the Cuban Revolution and the mass exodus that followed, to recent migratory waves, Cuban-Americans have transformed the landscape of many Florida cities, especially Miami, and have played a crucial role in U.S. politics.

The first Cuban exiles who arrived in the United States in the 1960s were mostly professionals and middle-class individuals fleeing FIDEL CASTRO'S communist regime. These immigrants brought with them a strong culture of political participation, which, over time, translated into significant influence on the U.S. political scene. As the community grew, so did its electoral power and its ability to elect leaders who defended its interests in Congress.

Today, Cuban-Americans are represented in both major U.S. political parties, and their leaders have influenced policy formulation on issues as diverse as foreign relations, immigration, human rights, and the economy.

But before exploring their successes, it is important to understand the context of Cuban immigration that led to the strengthening of this community in the country.

The first wave: Refugees after the cuban revolution (1960-1970)

The first wave of Cuban immigrants began after the Cuban Revolution of 1959, led by FIDEL CASTRO. Thousands of middle and upper-class Cubans, many of them professionals and entrepreneurs, left the island to escape political repression, property confiscation, and the lack of freedoms under the new communist regime. Miami quickly became the main destination for these exiles, laying the foundation for the consolidation of a strong Cuban-American community in South Florida.

During this period, the United States facilitated the arrival of Cuban refugees through policies such as the Cuban Adjustment Act of 1966, which offered Cubans a fast track to obtaining permanent residence. The U.S. government, immersed in the Cold War, openly supported Cuban exiles as a way to oppose CASTRO'S communist regime.

The Mariel Crisis (1980)

The Mariel Crisis in 1980 marked another turning point in Cuban immigration. More than 125,000 Cubans left the island in a mass exodus when FIDEL CASTRO allowed those who wished to leave to do so through the port of Mariel. This wave was different from previous ones, as it included people from lower classes, former prisoners, and marginalized individuals by the Cuban regime. Although it initially caused tensions in Miami, over time, the "Marielitos" integrated into the growing Cuban-American community.

The Balsero Crisis (1994)

In 1994, Cuba faced a severe economic crisis, known as the Special Period, after the collapse of the Soviet Union, its main economic ally. The lack of resources caused widespread shortages, and many Cubans took to the sea in makeshift rafts, risking their lives to reach the shores of Florida. This exodus, known as the Balsero Crisis, led to the departure of more than 35,000 Cubans in just a few months.

To address this situation, the United States and Cuba signed migration agreements in 1994 and 1995, under which the United States would legally accept up to 20,000 Cubans a year, while Cuba agreed to curb unauthorized emigration. This also led to the establishment of the "wet-foot, dry-foot" policy, which allowed Cubans who reached U.S. soil to stay, while those intercepted at sea were returned to Cuba.

Impact of "Wet-Foot, Dry-Foot"

The "wet-foot, dry-foot" policy resulted in the arrival of thousands of Cubans over the next two decades. Many Cubans saw this policy as a safe gateway to the United States, and they continued to risk crossing the Florida Straits, despite the serious dangers involved.

Between 1994 and 2016, it is estimated that more than 650,000 Cubans settled in the United States, many of them in Florida. This period also saw the building of a strong Cuban diaspora in cities like Miami, which became a bastion for Cuban-Americans and a center of political and economic influence.

End of "Wet-Foot, Dry-Foot" (2017)

In January 2017, shortly before leaving office, Barack Obama ended the "wet-foot, dry-foot" policy as part of an effort to normalize relations between the United States and Cuba. This marked the end of an era in Cuban migration policy and created uncertainty for those still seeking to emigrate.

After the policy change, many Cubans have continued trying to reach the United States, but through other countries, using routes through Central America and Mexico, where the migration situation has become more complex. The end of "wet-foot, dry-foot" meant that Cubans no longer had a guaranteed path to stay in the United States, making it more difficult for those seeking asylum.

Current Crisis and Recent Waves 2024

In recent years, particularly since 2021, the economic crisis and political repression in Cuba, exacerbated by the COVID-19 pandemic, have triggered a new surge in emigration. In 2022, record numbers of Cubans attempted to cross the U.S.-Mexico border, with more than 220,000 Cubans trying to enter through that route in that year alone.

Cubans have opted for this route due to the restrictions imposed by the end of the "wet-foot, dry-foot" policy and the difficulties in legally emigrating. Many first arrive in Nicaragua, a country that does not require a visa for Cubans, and then cross Mexico in an attempt to reach the United States.

Cuban-American political power

Over the decades, Cuban-Americans have not only integrated into U.S. society but have also achieved a very impactful political influence. One of the most prominent examples of this influence is the Díaz-Balart family, whose members have held key positions in the United States Congress and have played an important role in U.S. and Latin American politics, particularly concerning Cuba. Here is a brief overview of some of the most recognized Cuban-American politicians.

Lincoln Díaz-Balart

Lincoln Díaz-Balart, was one of the pioneering Cuban-American politicians in Congress. Born in Havana in 1954, he came to the United States with his family after Fidel Castro came to power. Lincoln was elected to the House of Representatives in 1992 for Florida's 21st district, where he served until his retirement in 2011. During his time in Congress, he was known for his strong opposition to the Cuban regime and his advocacy for human rights and democracy in Cuba. Lincoln was a key defender of the Cuban Adjustment Act and played an active role in shaping U.S. policy toward Cuba.

Additionally, LINCOLN DÍAZ-BALART was the promoter of the NACARA law, enacted in 1997, which provided immigration relief to citizens of Nicaragua, El Salvador, and Guatemala who came to the U.S. escaping civil wars and dictatorships in their countries. Aside from his fight against the CASTRO regime, LINCOLN DÍAZ-BALART was and remains highly influential in the Cuban-American community and is considered one of the architects of the Cuban-American coalition that has maintained a strong and cohesive political position in Florida.

MARIO DÍAZ-BALART

LINCOLN's younger brother, MARIO DÍAZ-BALART, has also had a successful political career. Born in Fort Lauderdale in 1961, MARIO has represented several districts in Florida in the House of Representatives since 2003. Like his brother, MARIO has been a staunch advocate for a hardline policy toward the Cuban regime and has called for strengthening sanctions and international pressure to promote change on the island. MARIO has been particularly active on foreign policy, immigration, and economic issues, and has played an important role in Florida politics, a key state both in presidential elections and in discussions about policy toward Latin America. His ability to forge bipartisan alliances and his deep knowledge of Cuban-American issues have made him a highly respected and influential figure within Congress.

ILEANA ROS-LEHTINEN

Along with the DÍAZ-BALART brothers, another prominent figure in Cuban-American politics has been ILEANA ROS-LEHTINEN. ROS-LEHTINEN was the first Latina and Cuban-American elected to the U.S. Congress in 1989, where she served until her retirement in 2019. During her time in Congress, ROS-LEHTINEN was a strong advocate for human rights and a fierce critic of the Cuban regime. Her leadership as chair of the House Foreign Affairs Committee made her one of the most powerful voices in U.S. foreign policy, particularly regarding Cuba and Latin America.

Chapter 6

Mequíades "Mel" Martínez

Mel Martínez was born in Cuba in 1946 and emigrated to the United States at the age of 15 as part of Operation Peter Pan, a program that helped thousands of Cuban children escape Fidel Castro's communist regime. His experience as a refugee profoundly influenced his political career and his commitment to immigration policies and freedom.

His political career began in Florida, where he was elected mayor of Orange County (1998-2001). Later, in 2001, he was appointed Secretary of Housing and Urban Development (HUD) by President George W. Bush, becoming the first Cuban-American to serve in a presidential cabinet. In 2004, Martinez was elected U.S. Senator for the state of Florida, becoming the first Cuban-American to hold a Senate seat. During his Senate tenure (2005-2009), Martinez worked on key foreign policy issues, especially in the fight against communism in Latin America, and advocated for immigration reform. In 2007, Martinez made history again by becoming the first Latino to chair the Republican National Committee (RNC), the body responsible for coordinating the Republican Party's electoral strategies.

Marco Rubio

Senator Marco Rubio, another prominent Cuban-American, has been one of the most influential figures in U.S. politics in recent years. Rubio, born in Miami to Cuban parents, was elected to the Senate in 2010 and quickly established himself as a leader within the Republican Party. In 2016, he ran for president, catapulting him onto the national political stage.

Rubio has been a key figure in immigration policy discussions and has maintained a hardline stance toward the Cuban regime, opposing the restoration of diplomatic relations between the United States and Cuba initiated by President Barack Obama. His conservative political vision and ability to connect with the Cuban-American community have made him a decisive figure both in Florida and nationally.

Other Cuban-Americans in high U.S. politics

BOB MENENDEZ

On the other side of the political spectrum, Democratic Senator BOB MENENDEZ, the son of Cuban immigrants, has been a prominent voice within the Democratic Party. MENENDEZ has served as a senator from New Jersey since 2006 and has been one of the most influential Latino leaders in Congress. Despite ideological differences with Republican Cuban-American leaders like RUBIO and the Díaz-Balart brothers, MENENDEZ has also been a staunch advocate for democracy in Cuba and has played a key role in U.S. foreign policy toward Latin America.

TED CRUZ

Another Cuban-American who has gained prominence in national politics is TED CRUZ, senator from Texas since 2013. Born in Canada to a Cuban father, CRUZ has been a prominent leader within the Republican Party's more conservative wing. His 2016 presidential candidacy made him an influential figure in national political debates. Like RUBIO, CRUZ has been a firm opponent of the Cuban regime and has promoted conservative policies on issues such as taxes, immigration, and individual rights.

ALBIO SIRES

ALBIO SIRES, born in Cuba in 1951, emigrated with his family to the United States in 1962. He was elected to the House of Representatives in 2006, representing New Jersey. Throughout his political career, SIRES has worked on foreign policy issues and has been a strong advocate for the Cuban community. SIRES has called for a firm policy toward the Cuban regime, promoting democracy and human rights on the island. In addition, he has worked on issues such as education, infrastructure, and social welfare in his district.

NICOLE MALLIOTAKIS

NICOLE MALLIOTAKIS, daughter of a Cuban mother and Greek father, was elected to the House of Representatives in 2020, representing New York's 11th district. As the daughter of a Cuban exile, MALLIOTAKIS has been a staunch opponent of the Cuban regime and has worked on foreign policy issues related to Latin America. Additionally, she has focused her work on local issues in her district, such as public safety, the economy, and infrastructure.

The political legacy and future of Cuban-Americans

Perhaps the greatest legacy of the Cuban-American community in Florida has been its political influence. Over the decades, Cuban-Americans have consolidated as a powerful and cohesive electoral bloc, especially in Miami-Dade County, where, as we have seen, they represent a large part of the electorate. This group has proven to be decisive in multiple elections, both at the state and national levels, and has been courted by major political parties, especially in presidential elections.

Cuban-Americans are largely responsible for Florida no longer being a swing state. Their ability to swing the vote in favor of one party or another at crucial moments is undeniable, and their political future seems unstoppable.

The political crisis in Venezuela and Its impact on migration to the United States

In recent years, one of the most significant factors contributing to the growth of the Latino population in the United States has been the political, economic, and social crisis in Venezuela. This South American country, once one of the region's most stable and wealthy democracies, has faced a series of deep problems that have led millions of Venezuelans to seek refuge in other countries, including the United States. The arrival of Venezuelan immigrants has transformed migration dynamics in some states and added a new layer of complexity to the Latino community in the country.

The political and economic collapse in Venezuela

Since the early 2000s, Venezuela has been immersed in a multifaceted crisis that has deeply affected the lives of its citizens. Under the governments of HUGO CHÁVEZ and his successor, NICOLÁS MADURO, the country has experienced a combination of political instability, growing authoritarianism, an economy in free fall, and the collapse of basic services. State-controlled economic policies, corruption, and the mismanagement of natural resources, particularly oil, have led to runaway inflation, shortages of food, medicine, and a severe humanitarian crisis.

As living conditions in Venezuela worsened, millions of people were forced to emigrate to seek safety, stability, and economic opportunities in other countries. According to the UN, more than 7 million Venezuelans have left the country since the start of the crisis, making it one of the largest migration crises in the world. While most Venezuelans have migrated to neighboring countries such as Colombia, Brazil, and Peru, a significant number have arrived in the United States.

Increase in Venezuelan migration to the United States

Venezuelan migration to the United States is not a completely new phenomenon; in the 1980s and 1990s, there was already a small Venezuelan community in cities like Miami. However, the crisis that began in the 2010s has led to an explosion in the number of Venezuelan immigrants arriving in the country.

One of the main reasons why many Venezuelans choose the United States is the existence of established communities, especially in Florida, where a significant diaspora already lived. Miami has become a refuge for many middle- and upper-class Venezuelans fleeing political persecution and economic deterioration in their country. In addition, access to economic opportunities and the possibility of obtaining asylum in the United States have been key factors in the decision to migrate.

Since 2014, the number of asylum applications filed by Venezuelans has grown exponentially. In 2018, for example, Venezuelans were the group that filed the most asylum applications in the United States, surpassing even countries with high levels of violence, such as El Salvador and Guatemala. As the situation in Venezuela worsened, the U.S. government has granted temporary protection to many Venezuelans through Temporary Protected Status (TPS), which allows beneficiaries to live and work legally in the country while it is not safe to return to their country of origin.

The impact of the Venezuelan community in the United States

The massive arrival of Venezuelans has had an undeniable impact on the dynamics of some cities and states, especially in Florida. Miami, in particular, has become a nerve center for the Venezuelan diaspora, where they have established businesses, communities, and support networks. The presence of Venezuelans has been visible in local culture, media, and, of course, politics.

Politically, Venezuelans who have arrived in recent years have brought with them a unique perspective, marked by their experience of living under an authoritarian regime. Most Venezuelans have shown a tendency towards the Republican Party due to their opposition to socialist governments in Latin America and the tougher stances some Republican politicians have taken towards regimes like that of NICOLÁS MADURO. This conservative approach has resonated especially in Florida.

In addition to politics, Venezuelan immigrants have also contributed to the local economy, especially in Florida and Texas, by establishing businesses and generating jobs. Many Venezuelans who came to the United States were professionals with advanced training or entrepreneurs who have used their skills and resources to quickly integrate into the U.S. economy. While they face the same challenges as other migrant groups, such as cultural adaptation and obtaining legal immigration status, their economic contribution has been notable.

The decisive Puerto Rican vote in Florida

Puerto Ricans make up a significant part of the Latino population in the United States, and their vote has become increasingly relevant in North American politics. Unlike other Latino groups, Puerto Ricans have U.S. citizenship by birth, as Puerto Rico is an unincorporated territory of the United States. This means that Puerto Ricans can vote in national elections if they reside in one of the 50 states or the District of Columbia, although they cannot vote in presidential elections while living on the island.

Puerto Rican voter demographics

There are approximately 5.8 million Puerto Ricans living in the United States, of whom an estimated 3.4 million are eligible to vote. Geographically,

Florida is the state that most hosts citizens from the Island of Enchantment. Although historically, New York has been one of the most important centers of the Puerto Rican diaspora, according to the 2020 Census, Florida is the state that hosts one of the largest Puerto Rican communities in the country, particularly in areas such as Orlando, Kissimmee, and Tampa. The Puerto Rican population has grown considerably in the last two decades, especially after Hurricane Maria. The Puerto Rican vote in Florida is seen as decisive in deciding elections, and it has proven to be so.

Senator RICK SCOTT's Victory, Puerto Rico decided!

In the 2018 Senate elections in Florida, RICK SCOTT, former governor of the state, achieved a very narrow victory over Democrat BILL NELSON, who had been a senator for more than 18 years. SCOTT won by a thin margin, obtaining about 10,033 more votes than Nelson out of a total of more than 8 million votes cast. This difference of less than 0.2 % reflected how crucial each voter group was, especially Latinos.

The Latino vote, and particularly the Puerto Rican vote, played a decisive role in this election. The Puerto Rican population in Florida had grown considerably, especially after Hurricane Maria in 2017, which caused an exodus of Puerto Ricans to the central region of the state, particularly to cities like Orlando and Kissimmee. Historically, Puerto Ricans tend to vote more for the Democratic Party, but RICK SCOTT made a significant effort to win over this community.

As governor, SCOTT traveled several times to Puerto Rico to show his support after the hurricane and advocated for increased federal funding to help with the island's reconstruction. This allowed him to capture a significant portion of the Puerto Rican vote in Central Florida, a group that had felt disappointed by the lack of action from the federal administration following the crisis in Puerto Rico. SCOTT was able to secure a high enough percentage of this electorate to tip the balance in his favor in such a close election.

In addition to the Puerto Rican vote, SCOTT also benefited from the Cuban-American vote, which has historically supported Republicans. In total, SCOTT obtained about 45 % of the Latino vote in Florida, an exceptionally high figure in a state where 17 % of the total electorate is Latino and in one of the closest elections in the state's recent history.

Conclusions

1. **Latinos have become a key voting bloc:** The Latino population has grown significantly, now constituting 19 % of the U.S. population according to the 2020 census. This demographic growth translates directly into political power, as more Latinos become eligible to vote, increasing their influence on national elections. Latino voters are no longer concentrated in the traditional states like California, Texas, and Florida, but have expanded to places like Georgia, North Carolina, and Nevada, reshaping the political landscape in those areas.

2. **Latinos are diverse in origin and political behavior:** The Latino population in the U.S. is not monolithic. While Mexican Americans make up more than 60 % of the Latino population, other groups like Puerto Ricans, Cubans, and Central and South Americans also hold considerable sway in different regions. This diversity leads to varying political behaviors, with factors such as country of origin, migration history, and generational status influencing voting patterns.

3. **Increased political engagement among latinos:** Over the last few decades, Latinos have steadily increased their political engagement, with turnout rising by 30 % between 2016 and 2020. The 2020 election saw approximately 16.6 million Latino voters, representing 13.3 % of the electorate. Despite this progress, voter participation among Latinos still lags that of other groups, suggesting room for growth in mobilization efforts.

4. **The rise of young latino voters:** One of the most promising trends is the rise of young Latino voters, who bring new energy and perspectives into American politics. With a significantly younger median age than other demographic groups, young Latinos are increasingly engaged in issues such as racial and social justice, climate change, and immigration, making them a powerful force in future elections.

5. **The latino vote is crucial in battleground states:** Latinos are playing an increasingly decisive role in swing states like Arizona, Florida, and Georgia. In recent elections, they have been pivotal in determining outcomes in tight races.

Final Chapter

There is great anticipation for the trends of the Latino vote in the 2024 election, with projections from NALEO (National Association of Latino Elected and Appointed Officials) expecting more than 17.5 million Latinos to vote, representing a 6.5 % increase compared to Latino participation in the 2020 elections. This means that more than 1 in 10 voters across the country will be Latino, underscoring the growing importance and influence of this community in U.S. politics.

In key states, the Latino vote will be crucial in deciding the outcome of the elections. In Arizona, approximately 855,000 Latino voters are expected, who could be decisive in a historically contested state. In California, more than 4.8 million Latinos are projected to vote, making this group an important voting bloc in the most populous state in the country. Florida will see more than two million Latino voters participate, consolidating its importance in both state and federal elections.

Other states where the Latino vote will also have a great impact include Texas, with nearly 3 million Latino voters; Nevada, with 280,000 voters; and Georgia, where 195,000 Latinos are expected to turn out at the polls. In the Northeast, New York will see the participation of nearly a million Latino voters, showing that this community is not only crucial in the southwestern and southern states but also in key regions of the Northeast.

This increase in Latino voter turnout is not just a sign of demographic growth but also a reflection of the power and influence this community has

Conclusions

gained in the U.S. political process. With each election, Latinos continue to demonstrate that they are a fundamental political force, capable of influencing the outcomes of very closely contested races.

Once the election is over and we have all the official figures on Latino voter participation and how it influenced the results, this data will be added to both the digital and print editions of this publication in a revised edition.

Available on Amazon
2024 Edition

Made in the USA
Columbia, SC
03 November 2024

45257654R00078